BROKEN BREAD

BROKEN BREAD

John Wright Follette

GOSPEL PUBLISHING HOUSE
Springfield, Missouri 65802

02-0474

[PRINTED
IN U·S·A·]

PREFACE

BROKEN BREAD comes to you as the result of many, many requests on the part of those who have listened to my preaching and teaching, dear friends who appreciate the truth and have a hunger for spiritual reality. They have asked me to publish some of the messages which they have heard and found helpful in interpreting and explaining their Christian experience.

These sermons were not prepared and written especially for this book. Rather they are stenographically reported from messages given by me at different meetings and in different places. Consequently I have not made any attempt to cultivate a literary style. And I have not made any particular arrangement or selection of the material used. Many of these messages appeared in three little devotional books I published some time ago: *Broken Bread, Old Corn* and *Fruit of the Land.* They have been of great value to hundreds.

Readers of these books report that they enjoy rereading, studying and feeding upon the different phases of truth presented. They often say that upon the second or third reading of some message they discover fresh insights and meanings in the Word.

Some may find the teaching elementary, while to others it may be a bit revolutionary. I trust all will find it illuminating and helpful. Accept the portion which is adequate for you in your present place of spiritual culture and development. Let the truth work in you. I pray that you may give way to the inner urge and thirst for truth, for God, and for reality. This inborn thirst for truth has taken me past the masks and husks of materialism and that which is purely natural into a vast realm of spiritual reality. It has helped me to make many definite discoveries in the field of spiritual revelation.

In teaching I seek to interpret the truth in the simple prosaic forms of everyday life. Truth is not only to be believed; it is to be lived. It is never truly our own until it is personalized and, in objective fashion, becomes a part of our personality. Thousands may believe, giving mental assent—and often with quite an emotional reaction—but the truth never becomes manifest in their life and character.

Therefore I pray that the lessons and material found here may bless and feed you. May they lead you on to a fuller understanding of life and the power to interpret it. May they indeed be "broken Bread" from my bread basket to instruct and encourage you in the growth and development of your Christian character.

—John Wright Follette

New Paltz, New York

CONTENTS

TROUBLE IS A SERVANT

All of us know trouble—at least I hope we do;
Trouble is a servant, but known as such to few.
We are taught to shun her and, if she comes too near,
Seldom do we face her but run away in fear.
Good and bad must meet her, the universe around—
Sinners, saints, kings and knaves—she comes where man is found.
Always make her serve you, for she can serve you well;
Just HOW you may use her your life will always tell.
Trouble is but passive—it's by our power to will
We make her either bless us or do the soul some ill.
How do you translate her from phrases filled with pain
To messages of strength—from loss to endless gain?
By faith we see behind the outer frightful mask
A servant in disguise, to do a gracious task.
Hearts may feel her wounding and life may suffer loss;
Faith translates her working, as freeing gold from dross.
Trouble will discover to any yielded heart
Hidden depths of power it only knew in part;
Sympathizing power, and love that understands;
Strength to help another with trouble-tested hands.
Trouble will release you from self and make you kind,
Adding new dimensions to heart and soul and mind.
Do not shun this servant, but look beyond her task
To beauty she will work—for which you daily ask.
Always see in trouble a chance to grow in grace,
Not a stroke of evil to hinder in your race.
Live the life triumphant above her fiery darts;
Rich fruitage will be yours to share with needy hearts.

—John Wright Follette

I.

TROUBLE—A SERVANT

DID you ever test yourself as to how you react to trouble or tragedy? In life's school we often find that God uses trouble or misfortune to prove our faith or to test our character. Trouble has a way of stalking down the road and meeting us so many times when we least expect it.

I am sure we all know that such proving or testing may befall us without our being personally or directly the cause of it. Many, many times it is beyond our control. If it were otherwise we should probably avoid all such testings and keep to an easy, smooth path. But we should remember that trouble, as well as the hours of sunshine and music, is a part of the divine arrangement and has a place in our program. Trouble and severe testings are not necessarily a sign of sin, failure, or lack of spirituality. They are often a sign of spirituality and growth which God must test and prove, for we are His workmanship.

Many people have the notion that the life of the Christian is, or should be somewhat charmed, void of trouble, testing, tribulation and suffering. Such people have shaped up for themselves, or hold as an ideal of real Christian living, an impossible or unscriptural conception as an objective.

Where in the world such people, so bewitched, have been living all these years, or what books they have read, is beyond me! Surely they do not know history, Christian

1

experience or the Bible. For all these keep ever before us the truth that *"Man is born unto trouble, as the sparks fly upward"* (*Job* 5:7). *"Many are the afflictions of the righteous but the Lord delivered him out of them all"* (*Ps* 34:19). *"For our light affliction, which is but for a moment, worketh for us a far more exceeding and eternal weight of glory"* (*2 Cor.* 4:17). *"Yea, and all that will live godly in Christ Jesus shall suffer persecution"* (*2 Tim.* 3:12). *"In the world ye shall have tribulation: but be of good cheer; I have overcome the world"* (*John* 16:33). *"And not only so, but we glory in tribulations also: knowing that tribulation worketh patience"* (*Rom.* 5:3).

Surely on the basis of all these Scriptures, we as Christians know better than to pray for exemption from trouble, and since we know that in God's plan it is a part of our inheritance, let us not avoid its peculiar ministry.

History is replete with examples of lives wrecked because of ungraceful reaction to trouble. In spite of the accumulated experiences of the ages, and the wisdom and the philosophy of the seers, many still fail to recognize that behind her mask, trouble is a *servant* to assist us. Any other view is due to lack of vision and perspective in that range. Too many see the immediate, the local, and interpret life and relative questions from a circumscribed viewpoint. The Scriptures say, *"While we look not at the things which are seen."*

As Christians, after we are convinced in our hearts that trouble is not designed to defeat us, is not a mere nuisance or cruelty, but is one of the corrective elements in great living, we must needs *learn how* to use it. How many problems would be solved and shipwrecks of faith be avoided could we take a positive, constructive attitude and see that trouble is one of the agents and mighty instruments placed in our hands for the shaping of character and the releasing of potential power for correct and glorious building!

How do you use trouble? Naturally, because of physical and fundamental elements in our make-up, we shun pain, discomfort and trouble. But that is because we relate them purely to their action upon the physical or upon the present mood. Many times hours are spent in praying away trouble, the great servant. At times we take long, circuitous journeys to avoid meeting her. Finally, when we are compelled to meet her, we spend a long, long time telling her or God that we do not like her and we wonder and wonder why we ever had to meet her. But trouble is not to be reasoned with; she is utterly unreasonable. She is to be *used*.

Please disabuse your minds of the erroneous thought that if you are good or a real spiritual Christian, totally yielded and consecrated, your life is therefore to be a charmed one and that God will spare you from trouble or disappointment. No, to reach such a fine place of consecration and yieldedness is only to make you a fit candidate for tribulation.

Tribulation is a word God uses in relation to saints. The etymology of the word means *threshing*. The farmer does not thresh weeds; he threshes the golden wheat that the grain may be separated *from* the chaff and the sticks. He is after grain, not trying to pound out some straw. Therefore God says, *Tribulation worketh patience*; that is, the golden grain of patience, long-suffering and kindness, comes by way of threshing or tribulation. Think of the splendid spiritual grain of character and noble living produced only through the tribulation process. The spiritual tone and quality of the mighty men of God came only through trouble and suffering.

In the world about us, in the fields of fine music, art and literature, the artist never reaches the climax of his

labors and gives to the world the best in creative beauty
and strength until he has known the poignant touch of
personal sorrow or grief or trouble. Oftentimes it is like
a divine alchemy turning the ordinary and prosaic life into
a glorious display of divine power, fortitude and beauty.
It is the *use* of trouble that releases the deeper springs
of our lives and sets aflow the streams of mercy and understanding which a perishing world needs.

Do not misunderstand me; I am not saying that trouble
alone makes us strong or noble or that it alone has a
transforming power. I am dealing with you as Christians
who believe Romans 8:28, and that text, as you see, is
never to be applied to lives which are not surrendered.
That is why many unsaved people never understand the
outworking of the Scriptures in the daily walk, but if the
Christian has anything remotely approaching the Spirit of
Christ, he can make trouble a servant to bring forth the
best in him. This I suggest in my poem, *Trouble Is
a Servant.*

But trouble in itself is neutral or passive; the whole
matter depends upon *how* we use it. One may take an
inactive attitude and lose the benefit of the trial; justify
himself, and trouble will make him bitter or resentful, or
it can make him hard, cruel and cynical. People who have
no faith, no perspective of thought or vision, let trouble
do all sorts of harmful and cruel things to them, but
thanks be to God there are many wonderful people upon
whom trouble has fallen who were able to see and to discern
behind its mask a servant at their beck and call, to build
them lives of strength and beauty.

In a simple study of such lives we find a certain creative power which makes out of their calamity a magnificent privilege. You have noticed in lives a twofold
reaction to trouble or tragedy: either it will break us in

spirit, melting the hardness and bringing us in our help-lessness to God, or it will throw us upon our feeble resources and human reasonings, and this in turn at times hardens us in spirit, makes us critical and often cynical. It robs the heart of the great privilege of trusting God and the developing of the life into rich and helpful avenues.

Trouble will make you either *bitter* or *better*. Notice how very much alike these words are, and how very little is needed to change them; just the letter *I*. Yes, dear ones, it is the *I* that changes the whole matter. When the *I* keeps out of the question, out of the difficulty, life will be *better*; but when the *I* is introduced and we get mixed in the trouble, life will become bitter and we hard. Too many times this *I* gets in the way; the poor, little, hurt *ego* gets a slap and down the street he runs, screaming for attention. The dear little *ego* sits in his doorway and weeps tears of self-pity until his eyes are so red and in-flamed that he just cannot *see* things as they are or should be.

It takes a quiet heart, peace of spirit, and clear vision (long range, if you please), to interpret trouble in terms of strength and high living. Little souls, small people, are usually hurt all the time; the *ego* within is unduly important and consequently is easily hurt or flattered. Such souls have too small a world and hence everything relates directly to the self within. They will have a very difficult time, to say the least.

Frequently such souls are persons who are seeking jus-tice, fairness, and a proper adjustment of life. They never seem to learn. We are not here for justice; we are here to *live*. If you expect to be a spiritual and victorious Christian, you may as well learn here and now to drop justice out of your vocabulary as far as it may relate to your life. We do not get justice *now*. God's Saturday night of settlement has not yet come.

Some live as though life and the Christian experience were some kind of slot machine: you put in a dime's worth of kindness and pull out three yards of blessing; then five cents' worth of charity and you think God *must* bless you next Saturday night. Be very good, kind or generous and next week the winds will blow you a fortune. It is true that what we sow that shall we also reap, and bread cast upon the waters shall return, but God is not too clear on the time element. So we shall not always receive our justice here and now.

Jesus never taught His followers to expect justice. Paul did not receive justice. Even great leaders in history did not always receive justice here and now. Do not mistake me; I do not mean that the Christian or the spiritually-minded one is not conscious of the hurt or the trouble of the injustice. Believe me, dear souls, the Holy Spirit makes one all the more sensitive to the pain, the hurt and the wrong, but the victorious soul has found the gift of grace and the love of God sufficient to hinder the trouble from marring his spirit.

The closer one gets to Christ the more sensitive he will be to pain, to little, petty, mean ways and all the train of unkind and unlovely things which would vex the heart and tarnish the spirit. The eyes are now anointed and he sees in them privileges of overcoming and high living. I am sure we have all lived long enough to have had some injustice done us. Yet today God has given us grace not to harbor any resentment or hard feelings. To have trouble or injustice and *know* the feeling of it, and yet live above and far from its damaging power, is a sign of real spirituality, a sign of Christian character He has wrought in the life.

Someone learned of a real *injustice* done me in material things one time, and he was horrified to know it came from a Christian source.

"Such treatment as that," he said, "is absolutely wrong. I would not stand for it."

Of course it was wrong and very unfair, and at times I was amazed and tried, but I kept my heart and life open for justice and the right thing to be done by me; however, I was neglected and seemingly forgotten. But God had taken me quite a long distance on the road and I knew He would take care of the matter; so I took of His grace and love and stood it. It never caused me a resentful spirit, nor did I allow the hurt and the disappointment to fester into a sore. And today I praise God for the realities of His life in my heart to keep it sweet when trouble and unfair dealings would chill it to indifference and hardness.

Had we time we could trace through history, both sacred and secular, scores of noble men and women who were *not* spared the hard places in life. They were good, moral, kind, noble, and yet came under the disciplinary measures of trouble. Certainly Paul knew trouble or he never could have written, *"In labours more abundant, in stripes above measure, in prisons more frequent, in deaths oft. Of the Jews five times received I forty stripes save one. Thrice was I beaten with rods, once was I stoned, thrice I suffered shipwreck"* (2 Cor. 11:23-25). Yet out of it all he comes purified and strengthened, a noble expression of God's grace and an example for the ages to come that trouble may be used to build a Christian character.

In the Old Testament we find Joseph and Job and many others demonstrating the same truth. Surely Joseph might have said, "All these things are against me. Where is God? Why all this confusion and trouble when He promised me great victory and triumph?" Yet listen to him after in faith he comes through, *"But as for you, ye thought evil against me; but God meant it unto good"* (Gen. 50:20). We are following in the steps of Christ, who said that the servant was not above his lord. And we read of Him, *"Though he were a Son, yet learned he obedience by the things which he suffered."*

What are you seeking in your trouble today? Is it *deliverance* or *development?* You may have the one and not grow, or you may have both and grow. Get the development first and the deliverance will be yours, too. Let this servant minister to you in a way no other servant can. Take the positive attitude and use your trouble as one of the most skillful and wonderful instruments God ever placed into your hands for the working out of the character of Christ to be duplicated in you.

Trouble, if correctly used, will bring you great peace and a deep surrender of spirit which nothing else can work in you. I have not gone far on the way but I can give as my personal testimony that these deeper revelations of truth and clear understanding of the things of God have come only through suffering. I cannot offer you any other method. May God grant you grace to take your share of trouble. Don't pray for exemption, but may He teach you and use this strange servant to build your life into noble proportions of strength and beauty, and from your life healing streams of understanding and love will flow to broken lives and timid, fearful hearts "For he who suffers most has most to give."

2.

THE CAMELS ARE COMING

THE story is found in the 24th chapter of Genesis.

The spiritual lesson I wish to bring to you from this story is based upon a dramatic and picturesque incident in the life of Rebekah; namely, her dealing with the camels. Therefore I will not go into detail with the beautiful analogy of spiritual truths we find in this wonderful chapter. The general teaching, I am sure, is familiar to most of us. However, we might suggest a few points of interest to build up a background of understanding for the camels and their part in the romantic adventure.

The first thing we notice in this story is the relation of the 22nd, 23rd and 24th chapters in their general teaching. Here we find a prophetic or dispensational pattern by way of illustration. In chapter 22 we have the story of the offering up of Isaac, then in chapter 23 the death of Sarah, and in chapter 24 the servant is sent forth to find a bride for him who in a way has been raised from the dead. These three chapters in a broad and sweeping way suggest God's movements in dispensational matters. Chapter 22 suggests the ministry and death of Christ, chapter 23 the setting aside of Israel, and chapter 24 the ministry of the Holy Spirit in calling out the Bride for Christ. It is well that we keep this divine program in mind lest we be tempted to inaugurate one suggested by over-anxious hearts who desire to *establish* a kingdom instead of *training* lives *for* a kingdom.

9

Acts 15:14-16—*"Simeon hath declared how God at the first did visit the Gentiles, to take out of them a people for his name. And to this agree the words of the prophets; as it is written, After this I will return, and will build again the tabernacle of David, which is fallen down; and I will build again the ruins thereof, and I will set it up."*

From the whole trend of prophetic utterance and prophecy already fulfilled, we see this is not a day or period for the material establishment of a kingdom, but the establishment of a kingdom in the hearts of His people. Especially is it the period of discipline and training of believers for a future ministry and fuller expression of life in a new age. Scriptures such as Eph. 1:3, 4 and Rom. 8:28, 29 suggest the lofty objective of the Spirit to conform and train.

In the story we find Abraham represents God the Father, while Isaac represents Christ, the Son, and the servant represents the Holy Spirit. One is tempted to relate suggestive bits of truth found in nearly every verse, but I will try not to give too much exposition and restrict the teaching to the camels. The first mention of them is in verse 10. *"And the servant took ten camels of the camels of his master and departed."* Here we find where the camels came from—they are a part of the equipment sent by Abraham. Then in verse 11 we find who has control of them. *"And he made the camels to kneel down without the city by a well of water at the time of the evening...."*

In passing let us notice it is the servant who takes the initiative in greeting and interesting Rebekah. *"No man can come to me, except the Father who hath sent me draw him"* (*John* 6:44). Also let us remember what momentous results may often hinge upon seemingly insignificant doings. Her act of courtesy in verse 18 and offer (spontaneous and from the heart) to water the camels opened the door to her romance and great blessing. Heb. 13:2—*"Be not forgetful to entertain strangers; for thereby some have entertained angels unawares."*

When we consider Rebekah as the called out Christian in training by the Holy Spirit for deeper fellowship with the heavenly bridegroom, we see many lovely bits of truth tucked away in the story. In verse 22 we find the servant begins to reward her—golden earrings, bracelets, and ten shekels of gold. Gold, as we know, always means divinity— the heavenly, divine qualities. The earrings tell us of devotion in loving service (Psa. 40:6), and also the listening ear (Psa. 45:10). Her ears are tuned to heavenly things. Hands suggest service; so the golden bracelets mean spiritual service rendered with correct motive and from the heart. The ten shekels of gold mean the divine nature of which she is now a partaker—the divine supply for her good. Again in verses 53 and 54 we are told of a further rewarding. Silver means redemption; so she has jewels of silver or the redemptive blessings of her bride-groom. Also jewels of gold or the divine blessings from heaven. The raiment suggests the covering she has in Christ's atonement—His righteousness now covers her.

The brother and mother receive "precious things." This is the overflow of blessing from God in any heart or community where Christ is truly enthroned. Many a home has been blest with "precious things" merely by the presence of a saved or consecrated member. So also has a nation been blest and honored by the faith of a few.

Let us note in verse 58 that the whole matter of Rebekah's going and the full flowering of her romance depended upon her personal answer. She said, *"I will go."* The whole matter is very personal and I am sure God wants it to be so. It was a great step of faith to be

sure. She had to leave kin and home and had really
never seen the lover to whom she was going. She must
trust implicitly in the faithfulness of the servant. *"Blessed
are they that have not seen and yet have believed."*

We now find another reference to the camels. Verse 61:
"...and they rode upon the camels ..." This brings us
more directly to the question of the camels and *what* they
mean. But before we can explain about them let us clear
up a few thoughts concerning the objective of this journey
and the design of the romance.

So far in the illustration we find the servant fully
represents both the person and work of the Holy Spirit
in this dispensation as He faithfully deals with the heart
in its quest for the heavenly bridegroom. Also Rebekah
pictures very well the Christian in his response to the
Holy Spirit and his hunger for Isaac, his beloved. Let
us remember, as Christians seeking deeper fellowship with
Christ and fuller revelation of His Word, that spiritual
life and Christian character wrought in us becomes the
means of appreciation of Christ and His bridegroom fellowship. The deep desire to see our Isaac and to be with
Him is in other words the deep desire for fellowship and
capacity for revelation. Therefore *whatsoever* deepens my
fellowship and gives me spiritual life and character will
be in turn the *means* used by God to carry my heart from
one phase to another and still another of spiritual understanding.

God must continually use means to bring my heart
from one plane or realm to closer relations and nearness
to Christ. The very means He uses will be such as will
build up my spiritual life and character. The stronger
the character and deeper the life in Him the nearer I
am brought to my adorable Lord, my heavenly Isaac. Thus
must I cherish every means He may use to bring me to

His side. According to the philosophy of God's Word in relation to the question of Christian character we find that the character built by the Holy Spirit is quite a different thing from the divine nature which comes to the believer when he is born again. One is a gift, the other a result of proving. Character is built by proving: trials, hardships, sorrow, trouble, and spiritual discipline.

Now I think we are able to understand *what* the camels are. In the story the camels were the means of locomotion to carry Rebekah from her home to Isaac, her beloved. So in our Christian life God sends a caravan of camels to carry us to our blessed Isaac. These are the manifold trials and testings to which we are subject. I know there are some who think there should be some other means to carry us to Isaac but God has so ordained it and there is no use quarreling with God or His divine arrangements or the laws of spiritual development. Prayer will never change these fundamental principles and laws. But prayer may and does help us in a quicker and more understanding adjustment and helps us to work with Him in the scheme. In verse 10 you will remember the camels were a part of Abraham's planning and were sent by him. To help you in this, read: Psa. 34:19; II Cor. 4:17; II Tim. 3:12; John 16:33; Rom. 5:3.

So let us not be foolish and pray for God to draw us nearer and bring our hearts to sweet fellowship and understanding of Isaac and then when He sends us a camel to carry us there want to *shoot* him. Never shoot your camels! What foolish creatures we are anyway! With one breath we pray God to draw us near, conform us to His image, and deepen our lives in God, and with the next breath we shout at the camel He has sent to answer our prayer. Don't you remember it is tribulation that worketh patience and not a sweet feeling at an altar service?

The story says Rebekah *watered* the camels—that is, she *accepted* them. What do you do with your camels? What a time we have explaining to God what these camels are and how they act. What a time driving them from our doors and asking God to chase them out of our yards. Listen! Never quarrel with a camel. They are *most* unreasonable. All they seem to know is to *drink*. And how much they can hold! Some seem to have *such* capacity! Remember, Rebekah watered ten.

Have you not seen many of these ungainly creatures reaching out their necks and asking for water? How many times do we have to go down to the well and let down our bucket for a good draught of love or longsuffering, a bucket of patience or kindness, understanding, submission, forbearance and what not? How some camels can drink! We wonder if there can be any end to their thirst. Yes, there is. For the sequel to the watering is found in verse 61—*"And Rebekah arose, and her damsels, and they rode upon the camels, and followed the man: and the servant took Rebekah, and went his way."* So you see there is always a sequel and an answer to the thirst and watering.

But you must remember Rebekah did not ride them until she had watered them. To ride is to mount and be *above* the camel—he is under. Do you understand? She now makes the camel to serve her and he becomes a means to carry her to Isaac.

The camels are awkward and not so very easy to ride. There is an art to it and the secret of it is this—move *with* the camel and do not try to resist his momentum. For that is already *established,* so all you have to do is to *yield* to the sway and movement of the camel and you will soon learn to ride. Never resist the camel's momentum, for if you do it will make you sick and you will have a very hard time of it.

To help you ride the camels God has provided saddles. He always has a saddle to fit any camel He sends you. Perhaps you have an old camel very hard to manage. He has taken seemingly barrels of drink, but at last you have *learned* how to water him and now you are about to ride. He may be in the form of a person who "just kills" you. He or she seems to grind on you so and makes you *nervous*, as you say, and out of patience. But now at last you have the victory and are able to ride him. You have drawn buckets and buckets of patience and longsuffering for him and at last you see God in the matter and have *willingly* served him. Don't water a camel with a *pout* in your spirit for that always creates thirst and it takes ever so much longer to finish him up. Sing a good song as you let down your bucket and you hear it splash in the well of His grace. In this way his thirst will soon be slaked; then go get the saddle and ride.

Run down to the barn of God's Word and on the wall called James on the 4th row and peg 6 you will find a good saddle: *"But He giveth more grace..."* Just strap that onto his back and ride off. You will be surprised to know how well that saddle fits and how much easier the journey will be. He is now taking you to Isaac.

Yonder I see another camel that has been in your yard for months. You have given him a drink now and then but not enough to really slake his thirst—just enough to keep him quiet. He is the long-drawn-out trial and one seemingly without reason. Have a good square look at him and deal frankly with him. Knowing now *what* he is just water him quickly and hie you to the barn again and get a saddle, for you are ready to ride him. On the wall of II Corinthians, row 9 and peg 8, is your saddle: *"And God is able to make all grace abound toward you:*

*that ye, always having all sufficiency in all things, may
abound to every good work.*" It is such a fitting saddle—
made to order—and so easily adjusted. Step in the stirrup,
sister, and ride on.

Near me here I find a poor, weak camel. He is very
wobbly and lame. He is the camel of your weak nature.
He got dreadfully crippled you know in "the fall" and
of course he never got over it. You always did want
him to be big, strong and healthy, but alas! the poor
creature at last developed knock knees. So now you are
called upon to water him. Remember he is to be ridden
and will take you a long, long way. So do not keep him
off in one corner of the yard hidden *behind* a tree. If
you do that he will always want a drink at the *wrong* time
and as sure as you are alive he will bellow when you want
a nice quiet time. Deal with him in all fairness
and honesty. Water him though he may take barrels and
barrels, for he is to be ridden. Go then to this wonderful
barn of God's Word. There on the wall of 2 Corinthians,
row 12 and peg 9, is one of the oldest and most famous
saddles. "*And he said unto me, My grace is sufficient
for thee: for my strength is made perfect in weakness.
Most gladly therefore will I rather glory in my infirmities,
that the power of Christ may rest upon me.*" I think
there must have been thousands of people who used this
saddle and yet there is not so much as a buckle broken
on it. Paul rode it a long time and it carried him safely
to his Lord.

And so they come, camels, camels, camels—there seems
to be no end to them. There is another one yonder, a
most evasive and uncertain creature. He just came from
behind a bit of shrubbery and you are not sure *what* he
is after. But perhaps you have learned how to deal with
this camel—Temptation. There is also a saddle for him

which perfectly fits his peculiar humps. On the wall of 1 Corinthians, row 10 and peg 13, is the one for him. *"There hath no temptation taken you but such as is common to man: but God is faithful, who will not suffer you to be tempted above that ye are able; but will with the temptation also make a way to escape, that ye may be able to bear it."*

And look! What is that poor, thin camel staggering along and so faint, not only from thirst but she is also hungry? And as we begin to feed and water her we are amazed at her capacity. This is the camel called Depression. How faithfully we have had to deal with her and how very trying she has been! And lo and behold, there is another little camel behind her called, Recession. He is just the offspring of the old camel. But, thank God, there is also a saddle for her, too—on the wall of Philippians, row 4 and peg 19, we find the very one we need: *"But my God shall supply all your need according to his riches in glory by Christ Jesus."*

Let me ask you—what is your attitude toward your camels? Can you interpret them in the light of His Word? Let it shine upon them and you will learn *how* to water them and not to quarrel with them. Do not drive them away or think the devil is back of every unhappy situation or trial in your life. Remember in the story it was Abraham who sent them and it was the servant who made them kneel down at the well. You have a well—what are you doing with it?

To deny the camels are here is foolish. Look at the next old, brown fellow and say: "Well, good morning, Mr. Camel, I see you are very thirsty." He will probably snort (but don't mind that or try to correct him. He is only a camel and often they do such things). "How much water do you take? Just stand still here and I will water you, for I know in turn you are to serve me and carry me on a most desirable journey. So you see I want to water you well. And, too, Mr. Camel, I notice you are very heavily laden. Your master packed all those trappings on you when he sent you. I need not ask you *what* they are, for I know already. They are the gifts and jewels and precious tokens of his love and also the exquisite coverings he has sent to charm me and to adorn me for his presence. You may look ugly and ask for much water but you can't fool me. You are a great blessing sent in disguise. What! Another bucket? Yes, yes, there is plenty of water and the well is full; I will soon have your thirst satisfied. You are but a test of my faith—I shall soon ride you." And so accept him, water him and ride him.

There is another thought I like about the camels. It is found in verse 64—*"And Rebekah lifted up her eyes, and when she saw Isaac, she lighted off the camel."* Isn't that beautiful? The lifted eyes tell a story. And it was when she saw Isaac she lighted off the camel. She was seeing *him* and not a camel or the rough road.

There is no other means of locomotion. Had Rebekah seen merely a dusty, thirsty camel she might have sent it away and thus ruined her wonderful romance. Do not defeat your own prayers and heart's desire by misinterpreting God's methods of character building and spiritual culture. Trials are the food of the overcomer. Did not Joshua and Caleb of old say in regard to the enemy— *"they be bread for us"?* Bread is food for building. I am sure they had the right slant on the proposition.

This lesson from the camels is rather a picturesque form of telling a deep philosophy of life. Suffering and discipline are here and are for our good and not to defeat us. Let us learn *how* to use the camels sent to carry us to our Isaac.

In verse 63 we are told, Isaac at eventide was walking through the field in meditation when he lifted up his eyes and beheld the camels coming. Is that not suggestive? The day is already far spent, the shadows of the evening are upon us, and the nations are wrapped in clouds of confusion. Our Beloved, too, is waiting. Long has He watched the movements on the old earth's stage and now in meditation while the twilight curtains fall, he looks for the returning camel train bringing His Bride. Outlined against the sunset of this dispensation may there be a caravan to please His expectant gaze. Shall we not then water our camels and ride them, knowing that they are only the means in God's hands of taking us to our beloved Isaac?

STRUCK DUMB

Struck dumb by God! how cruel seem the words
  And yet thrice blest the heart where falls the blow.
A life transformed is his who suffers thus,
  For it is given only such to know
The rapture of the mighty wings of faith
  Which elevate the soul to realms above,
Where pain is sweet and wounds give only joy.
  His soul is charmed—a captive held by love.

No more to trace the path by signs he sees,
  Be they beneath the noonday sun most clear—
Or dim because at dusk the shadows fall.
  For blinded thus by God he knows no fear.
His eyes are closed, and yet his vision fills
  With things celestial in transcendent light.
The glory of the unseen world is his
  Whom God makes blind to earth's fair day or night.

His ears are deaf, no longer does he hear
  Earth voices calling him from every side.
It matters not how sweet and clear they be—
  Or rough with threats—he does not turn aside.
To every sound made deaf—that he might hear
  The music of the infinite and know
The harmonies of God, for such are his
  Whom God makes deaf to voices here below.

Struck dumb! no longer is there gift of song,
  A silence fills his soul serene and deep.
The music of his lips is wasted breath;
  In place of song 'tis given him to weep.
His trembling lips are mute—and yet they speak,
  Healed now to sing because they kissed God's rod.
The song must live since it is born from death.
  Thrice blest indeed the man struck dumb by God.

—John Wright Follette

20

3.

THE STROKE OF GOD

"Remove thy stroke away from me: I am consumed by the blow of thine hand." Psa. 39:10

WE have in the text before us a part of a prayer of David. Under severe pressure and trial, when reason was unable to discern the purpose of the stroke, and faith was too feeble to trust, he cried out in distress, *"Remove thy stroke away from me: I am consumed by the blow of thine hand."* It is not my object to treat this verse textually and confine the message to God's personal dealings with the Psalmist, and perhaps trace out reasons why the Lord should desire to consume his strength. But rather let the text serve as a theme, "The Stroke of God." To many hearts no doubt this thought is not pleasing. God is revealed in His Word as a God of love and so the thought of His hand falling with a stroke upon one of His children may seem strange or even unkind. For this reason I trust the interpretation given in this message may help to clear the vision, quiet fears, subdue too quick judgment and inspire faith to trust an all-wise and tender Father.

The first thought suggested by these words, *The stroke of God,* no doubt brings to us the scene of Calvary. The rugged cross rises before us and again the story of God's judgment upon sin flashes across our minds. I trust it is so. For the first and supreme interpretation of these words centers here. God is holy—He hates sin. With no degree of complacency or shadow of compromise can He look upon it. Holiness and hatred of sin, like every other attribute, are living and active and must manifest themselves. His holy wrath at sin must strike. So to save humanity and to bring us to God, Christ not only bore our sins but He became sin that we might enter into salvation. He became the victim upon which the divine wrath, the judgment of God, struck. This is the story of the cross.

The picture of Calvary is given to us in prophecy:

"Surely he hath borne our griefs, and carried our sorrows: yet we did esteem him stricken, smitten of God and afflicted. But he was wounded for our transgressions, he was bruised for our iniquities; the chastisement of our peace was upon him; and with his stripes we are healed." (*Isa.* 53:4, 5).

The literal translation for the Hebrew, *hath laid upon* (v. 6) is, *caused to strike upon.* Therefore in considering the stroke of God upon the hearts of His children let us not confuse it with the thought of His judgment upon sin. Christ has successfully and satisfactorily met the judgment for our sins and paid in full the penalty required by the justice and holiness of God.

But there is another sense in which to consider this theme. It is not in relation to the sin question or the sinner, but has to do with the saints and especially those who are seeking deeper fellowship and conformity to the likeness and image of Christ. *"Struck dumb by God,"* were the strange words the Spirit brought to my heart over and over again as I was pondering this thought in relation to the saints.

In the natural we have all seen the unfortunate people whom we speak of as deaf, dumb and blind. The physical deprivation of hearing and sight is indeed a calamity. How thankful we should be that we are given the proper use of all our faculties! But thank God, today we are hearing of His marvelous work of healing power and many who have hitherto never seen, heard or spoken are being healed, and in answer to prayer and faith are entering upon the use of all their faculties. Such occurrences are indeed miracles and are truly wonderful to witness.

For a little while let us consider our *spiritual* natures and one of the many miracles God is performing for us in this realm of the soul and spirit. Do you know that the greatest miracles of God have not necessarily to do with the physical life? Such miracles as the healing of the deaf, dumb and blind and other marvelous works, because they are in the realm of the physical, appeal to the natural man and arouse unusual attention. The natural man desires to hear, see and feel, consequently the spectacular has a wonderful fascination for him. It excites his sense of wonder and amazement and leads him to delight and rejoice in the strange and unusual manifestation of the Holy Spirit. This condition is not only common today where the Lord is pouring out His Spirit in miracle working and signs and wonders, but in the days of Christ the same effect was produced. Because the people got their eyes upon the things seen, sought to please and gratify their sense life by the use of miracles, and rejoiced in the power and use of the same, the Lord was led to rebuke them and give them words of correction.

The next day after the miracle in which He fed five thousand the crowd continued to follow the Lord. What was the motive? Was it because of intense hunger for God and seeking of life? Were they starving in heart and longing for the bread of heaven? Not at all. Christ discerned their hearts and knowing the human desire merely to want the things that would appeal to their physical being, rebuked them.

"*Jesus answered them and said, Verily, verily, I say*

unto you, Ye seek me, not because ye saw the miracles, but because ye did eat of the loaves, and were filled. Labor not for the meat that perisheth, but for that meat which endureth unto everlasting life. . . ." (John 6:26, 27).

Let us not deceive ourselves. The fact that thousands press their way to the scene of miracles is no sign that they are hungry for God. Would to God they were! When the miracle fails to lead one past the satisfaction of human hunger or physical relief and does not bring him in touch with the bread of life, it has lost its purpose.

Christ saw the frailty of the flesh and the tendency to rejoice in power when it moved upon the natural, and wrought signs and deliverances unusual and marvelous. Therefore He sought to lift their vision, and to bring them into another realm where they might witness and rejoice in miracles of moral and spiritual value. That is why He speaks as He does in Luke 10:19, 20.

"Behold, I give unto you power to tread on serpents and scorpions, and over all the power of the enemy; and nothing shall by any means hurt you. Notwithstanding, in this rejoice not, that the spirits are subject unto you; but rather *rejoice, because your names are written in heaven."*

The fact that power was given to the seventy to triumph over sickness and disease was truly wonderful, divine! But to triumph over man's nature, his sin and moral condition, was more lasting. Even the sick whom Christ healed died at last. A miracle upon the physical or natural plane is, after all, fleeting and vanishes. Not so in the realm of the Spirit. The miracle wrought every time a soul is born again, or when God by His Spirit triumphs over the old creation and brings a trusting heart into a fuller realization of the divine life, is lasting and endures through the ages to come. To rejoice in the fact that

God has touched my physical body and wrought a miracle
(which fact is true) is one thing but to know that my
name is written in the Lamb's book of life and that
I am born of God is greater.

Why is it that it is harder to realize this truth and to
enter into spiritual phases of the subject of miracles as
Christ desires us to do? Is it not due to the fact that
(as Christians even) we are too much creatures of sense?
God has given us the body in which we tabernacle or
dwell. We are given five senses which act as reporters
to us concerning the world in which we live. We see,
hear, smell, taste and the natural man conducts his life
accordingly, orders his steps and lives what we call the
natural or physical life. These senses were in the original
purpose of God, no doubt, to act as servants or aids to
us, but since the fall, the physical has triumphed until
today as a rule, man is held a prisoner to his sense life.
This is the hindrance which we have from our ancestors
and is sometimes called our old creation. It is governed
by sight or the report of our senses.

The spiritual life is supernatural or *above* the natural.
We are now, as Christians, introduced into another realm,
elevated by the Spirit on to another plane where faith is
the governing law or power. It is the work of the Spirit
in our lives today to bring us out from the bondage and
control of the old life, physical and natural, and to adjust
us to God so that we shall truly live and move and have
our being in God, or as the Word says, *be seated with
Christ in the heavenly places.*

This does not mean that we are to become fanatical
and disregard the body which God has given us and by
unwise rules and extreme and foolish procedure try to
extricate ourselves from the natural life with all of its
activities. We are to recognize the body as our only vehicle

or medium of expression in life. Even Christ bore the human frame. We are to let it serve us as an *accommodation* while our souls are in training and our spiritual life is maturing for the next age. We are to regard the body and its needs and seek to glorify God in the same. *"For ye are bought with a price; therefore glorify God in your body, and in your spirit, which are God's"* (1 *Cor.* 6:20). But to let the laws of the natural and the life of the physical dominate is deadly to all spiritual development.

Think you it is a small matter that God is able to take a person born of the earth, bound by its laws, and held under the power of the old creation system, and by His marvelous work of the Spirit so transform him and bring him into the life of the Spirit that he can fellowship with his God? This is indeed a miracle!

In order to do this God must bring us as Christians seeking the deeper life, more and more out from under the bondage of the natural. We are to walk now by faith. Therefore He strikes, as it were, a blow at the sense life. As we yield to the Spirit and walk by faith He delivers us more and more from its control. He seems to delight to make the cross to triumph over every phase of the old creation.

In the beginning in the garden of Eden it was through the sense life that Satan made his appeal to Eve. Of course it was not primarily the physical act of Eve's eating the forbidden fruit which caused the fall. Eve consented in her *will* and the moment she thus consented, Satan triumphed in the surrender of her soul. The literal act of eating the forbidden fruit was merely the outward expression and enactment of the moral and spiritual failure within. The sense life was the approach—she saw, heard and tasted.

Now, in the deliverance of the cross, the victory consists in triumph over the sense life so that we are no longer moved by its reports no matter what its messages may convey, be they pleasing or threatening. If we are to walk in the new creation and maintain a spiritual life with its proper development, we are to be blind to the things seen, deaf to the voices of earth and dumb as far as speaking our words of judgment are concerned. This is why God seeks to make us, as it were, deaf, dumb and blind. What leaps and bounds God's people would make in the new life were they to yield to God's stroke and suffer the crucifixion of the old life!

In thinking of this theme the Spirit brought to my memory the picture of Christ as the perfect servant. This type of the Lord is so suggestive in connection with this study. Isaiah 42:19, 20—*"Who is blind but my servant? or deaf as my messenger that I send? who is blind as he that is perfect, and blind as the Lord's servant? Seeing many things, but thou observest not: opening the ears, but he heareth not."*

Here the Lord is presented to us in a very unusual character. The perfection of the servant lies in the fact that He has suffered the stroke of God and no longer sees, or hears from the human side of life. Never would the Lord Jesus have lived the life of victory and faith filled with its untold pressure, pain, disappointments, burdens, and tragedies had He not been blind to the many things seen by the natural eye. Time is too short to rehearse the different incidents in His life when He saw many things but observed them not. Think of Him in the wilderness in those hours of stress and temptation when the enemy *"showeth him all the kingdoms of the world and the glory of them."*

But there was victory! Christ was blind to the appeal of the flesh. And with the eyes of devotion, consecration and faith He looked beyond, beyond, BEYOND where His vision was filled with the glories of the kingdom to be won through suffering, pain and death. He saw the ultimate purpose of His earthly life glorious in the effulgence of eternal light. Struck blind that He might see beyond time into the heavenlies, gazing continually at eternal values.

I will mention another time when I am sure He was blind to the things seen. It was at the hour of His departure from the little group of disciples and followers. He had finished His work and poured out His life and now the only means left to carry on the tremendous work of evangelizing the world was a little group of helpless, uneducated and fainting disciples. There was no possible support from the political world, no social eminence to give prestige and influence, no one with money or material schemes—rather a little group of outcasts, despised, rejected and scorned, already showing signs of failure and cowardice.

But again there is victory! Blind to any material hopes or possibilities, Christ lifts up His eyes. Blind indeed! but most powerful in penetration and vision. He was able to leave them in faith because He saw God in the power of the Holy Spirit coming with heavenly life, supernatural power and possessing His followers. He saw them no longer as weak creatures of flesh but now transformed by the grace and power of God. They were the torch bearers of the light of heaven. He saw them scattered and persecuted but as flames burning their way down through the centuries. He saw the material nations rising, falling and perishing; but the light and the life which He had brought, continued to burn and blaze and triumph in unspeakable glory. Blind indeed! but piercing the darkness of centuries.

Christ, the true and faithful servant, was deaf. Time will not permit us to note the occasions when, with ears

closed to voices of earth, He moved in matchless grace
and victory. Hearing the groan of creation, the taunts
of Satan, the suggestions of the flesh, He yet lived in
perfect and absolute victory. Even when a voice assumed
the tender and attentive tone of affection as expressed
by Peter when he sought to spare the Lord the suffering
and humiliation which was ahead of Him, He was deaf.
"Be it far from thee, Lord, this shall not be unto thee."
His ears were deaf to suggestions which would hinder
His onward movement. The cross was the goal of His
earthly pilgrimage and no voice was to call Him aside
from the steps which led in the will of God. Or should
a voice in anger roar and threaten to frighten and in-
timidate, it mattered not for He was deaf. Yea, deaf!
but so attuned to God that His soul caught the harmonies
of heaven and the simplest words or wishes of His Father.

The Lord spoke the words of eternal life and yet at
times He was dumb. He triumphed completely over the
realm of the sense life. How many times when from
the natural He might have with one word silenced the
oppressor or vindicated Himself in many ways, He re-
frained from speaking! Many times He stood the contradiction of sinners, heard the rebukes of those who scorned,
and taunts of the enemy, yet the record reads, *"And he
opened not his mouth."*

Think of Him in the garden on the eve of the betrayal.
The group of followers sodden in sleep and He alone
in silent vigil. Then what an unusual and striking figure
He makes in the deep shadow of the olive trees, standing
alone, silent, serene and majestic while near at hand was
the cowardly, vulgar crowd, pressing upon Him, jeering
and taunting Him. The uncertain glare and flickering
flame of the torches reveal a majestic personage, un-
daunted and possessed of heavenly peace. The crowd draws

closer but is repulsed. They cower; they slink back, heads down and spiritless.

Again He triumphs! By *words?* Never! This is no time for vindication and defense of eloquence! He is silent. Struck dumb! This serves as a most profound rebuke. The effect is so startling that He Himself has to ask their purpose in coming. Dumb! but with a dumbness profound enough to triumph over flesh and hell. This is but a simple and hurried picture of the servant, deaf, dumb and blind, as it were, to triumph over the natural and make possible a victory for all who let a similar stroke separate them and bring them into the life of the Spirit.

Many wonder *why* the transformation, separation and development cause such pain and unrest at times. Many of you may not enjoy the explanation I offer but it is all I know. Where there is life there is movement, be it tremendous or most delicate and simple. Life seeks expression and resents death,—that is perfectly *natural*. When the stroke of God falls upon us and He seeks to blind our eyes that we may walk by faith, we resent it. The natural man wants a sign, a vision, a miracle, and to be *weaned* from them pains him.

Is it not the voice of the carnal man that says, "Let me *see* and I will believe"? The *new* man says, "I *believe*, therefore do I see." God reaches down, seeking to put His fingers over our ears lest we might hear sounds that distract us and would at times contradict our faith, but too often we are fearful and cry to hear. Again He lays His fingers upon our lips, (the check of the Spirit, I call it), and again what trouble we have. We feel we must tell this, or explain that. Talk! talk! talk! I do not know of a more deadly influence upon the spiritual life than that of talking. We are too loquacious for our spiritual good. How common

it is to hear such expressions as, "Did you hear?" "Did
you see?" "I heard." "Have you seen?" "Do you believe?"
and "Why do you suppose?" This is one way of feeding
the sense life and keeping it in a flourishing condition.

I have been surprised at a lack of faith on the part of
what we call spiritual people, sanctified and baptized
and candidates for translation. I mean a lack of faith
in this sense. They seem yet, in a great measure, dependent upon a sign or movement upon the physical or sense
life in order to stimulate them to believe God. I am also
surprised to see how wonderfully God *dares* to disap-
point them in their seeking.

Over and over again we hear reports from the foreign
field that God is working thus and so in marvelous healing
upon the raw heathen. Or again in our home country
hundreds of people (many times sinners and untaught
people) are being healed and delivered. Many and many
a time in the same meeting a saint of God who has been
seeking healing or deliverance for years, and is no doubt
pious and dutiful, cannot seem to get a touch from God;
and yet a sinner who knows nothing of the deeper things
walks in and at once receives.

I will suggest only one reason for this. The sinner is
on one plane—that of the flesh and physical—and God
caters to him for there is no other approach; and his
faith being simple God knows it and performs, maybe
even a miracle. The child of God, seeking a touch, is
on another plane. He is saved and has been introduced
into the realm of the Spirit. God is now seeking in this
child something far greater than mere faith for healing.
Healing is not the greatest thing in the experience of the
Christian. It may be that God is seeking to do a bit of
spiritual disciplining (something the sinner knows nothing
about). He does not want to cater to the sense life and

deal with His child as a sinner and so does not give him the satisfaction (by way of feelings) that he may have had before. God wants him to believe His Word only and test his faith in the silent places of life.

People classified themselves in this matter in the days of Jesus. John 14:11—*"Believe me that I am in the Father, and the Father in me: or else believe me for the very works' sake."* He wanted them to believe His *Word* first. If some had to have the works it was all right; but these latter belonged to the second class. Even in the matter of tongues—*"Wherefore tongues are for a sign, not to them that believe, but to them that believe not...."*

As Christians we should not have to have the same treatment that the sinner gets. I do not mean that the sinner does not have to have faith. Both have to have faith but they are on different planes and God deals with them accordingly. To believe Him for His Word's sake is what He wants. Therefore He may strike a blow to the sense life of His child and lead him to truly triumph by believing the Word only, when everything in the flesh realm contradicts the statement of truth. The sinner may need a sign to convince and help him on but I think as Christians we are to hold to the naked Word and let our sense life suffer the stroke of God.

In thus dealing with the saint in seeming delays, testings, and trials God is maturing him in the things of the Spirit. He seeks to bring us from the plane of the little child where we have to have *every* prayer answered *at once* or a sign or a miracle to coax us along. Why not let Him work a miracle upon us today? Maybe not a miracle for the physical eye to behold, but no less a miracle and one far more lasting. To deal thus with a babe in Christ would no doubt stumble him, but God is seeking grown-up sons whom He dares to prove, test,

and bring into deeper life in the Spirit. Did God deal
with grown sons as He does with babes and sinners, with
signs and quick answers to prayers—where would the
trial, patience, maturing and victory of our faith come in?

Friends, we are in the school of the Spirit. He is
working upon us with most infinite and patient care to
bring us into a life as far removed from the physical
as the Spirit is above the natural. Are we willing? No
one in himself is able. It took the power of the Holy
Spirit to bring Jesus through in perfect victory. Thank
God we have the same Spirit now dwelling in us. Therefore
when we feel the stroke of God blinding our eyes, closing
our ears, and sealing our lips, shall we not yield?

God is today working a mighty miracle upon His children.
It may not find its expression in the realm of the physical
in signs and wonders. It is in the realm of the Spirit
and is of quite a different character. It requires faith,
and that of a superior quality, to suffer the stroke of
God needed to close the eyes of the old life and to translate
us into the realm of true vision. Maybe the very hindrance today in your development of spiritual life is due
to the fact that you are seeing too many things, people,
conditions, acts, circumstances, symptoms, etc. If God seeks
to lay His hand upon your eyes and does not explain
to the satisfaction of your flesh the reasons for so doing,
then go blind. Remember, as the vision of the natural
leaves, the heavenly dawns. Maybe you are hearing too
much. The mind and heart are distressed because they
are not able to make a satisfactory reconciliation between
conflicting reports. God has not asked you to do so. All
He has asked is that He might place His fingers over
our ears lest we might be distracted by the sounds; and
it is only thus that we hear the voice of God and
"the sound of his goings."

Maybe you are too talkative. Many times we take the burden of explaining the universe. It is a waste of breath. Man's words are not used in the realm of the Spirit; the language there is from lips first struck dumb. Let us learn the bliss of silence. As sanctified, yielded Christians, we may well rejoice to know that already the pressure of His hand is upon our lives. God forbid that because we do not recognize its purpose we shall find ourselves praying, "Remove thy stroke away from me; I am consumed by the blow of thy hand." But now discerning the purpose of such a stroke shall we not cherish it and even through tears say, "The good hand of God is upon me."

4.

THE PRAYERS OF THE PRODIGAL

WISH to share with you some of the thoughts suggested by reading once more the story of the prodigal son as told by Luke in the fifteenth chapter of his Gospel. This incident makes rich appeal to almost anybody, good or bad, rich or poor, old or young, experienced or otherwise, purely on the basis of its very human and natural elements. It is colorful and intensely dramatic; perhaps that is the reason it so interests the minds of young people.

I am sure we have all heard messages based upon this narrative, and are familiar with the usual interpretation and application of truth and the salutary moral lessons deduced. Tonight, I do not wish to trace the lines of thought from the usual points, but rather share with you the bread of truth as I have found it tucked away in the story—fully as suggestive and instructive as the stereotyped lessons often drawn.

I have already suggested the theme for this meditation in the subject, "The Prayers of the Prodigal." At once we stop at the thought of prayer in connection with the prodigal, for one does not usually think of the prodigal praying. As a rule he is held up as an example in all the shame of his weakness and sin, but never do we picture him praying, and that twice.

Shall we review together the account and familiarize our minds with the general structure of it, so we may more fully appreciate *why* and *for what* he prays? We find here a typical home. It need not be only the one mentioned here, but may be duplicated a thousand times over our countryside. The characters and conduct are essentially the same there or here, then or now.

We do not know how long these two brothers have lived happily together, sharing the common blessings of the home and enjoying the fellowship of each member. But the time is reached (sooner or later by all) when the discovery of self-expression comes, with a keen desire to venture out upon life, to experiment and try out many potentialities of being. The thrill of a new step and the responsibility and joy of being on one's own, as we say, captivates this younger brother.

Let us here be tolerant. The two boys are evidently of very different temperament and disposition. Life appeals to each from very different angles. And surely there is nothing wrong in this. If the older son is satisfied to remain at home, continue in the general routine and perhaps prosaic life (at least to the younger son), let him stay. He is no doubt contented to go and come, come and go, and live out the life for which he seems fitted. Perhaps his gifts and callings are lodged in that field, and he would prove a great misfit did he try to adapt himself to a realm or condition for which he has neither capacity nor experience.

Nor shall we condemn the younger son. I am neither defending him nor excusing him. I do want to be fair and understand him. He may have been spoiled because he was the younger, as sometimes happens. That, however, would be the fault of the parents. At any rate he has quite a different make-up from his brother, and for this he cannot be blamed. He begins to find within and ever pushing through to manifestation in life, a thousand unsatisfied desires and promptings. He may have been, shall I say blessed or cursed, with an imagination? I will leave that for you to settle. At least he feels certain desires stirring; the Spirit of romance and adventure common to youth give him a sense of crampedness; and a great hunger fills his heart to get out, out, out—ever *out*.

He dislikes the confines of the natural environment and its limitations. The robust, visionary, throbbing life wants to try its wings. He feels the pull of the free, sunny air; he sees the blue sky of youth, the distant hills, green and luscious. Yes, they are green (just as green as inexperienced youth). But the dear lad does not know that. And do not try to tell him unless you wish to have war and trouble.

If you wish to help him, I trust God may give you grace, love, understanding and sound judgment. Try to see from his viewpoint. He has no background of experience as yet to help him, and so he is not capable of very sound judgment on many issues. He has not yet learned (as a Christian) the difference between possibility and probability. It takes some people a long, long time to learn this. Some seem never to learn it.

Do not quarrel with nature. Meet the condition as it is, honestly, and help the boy make the decisions necessary from his own heart, because *he wants* to do so. Do not buy him and worse still, do not force him to do the right, because you think if he does *not* he will break your heart. Never mind *your* heart. It is *his* heart you are after.

A most interesting question of motives comes in here, and I am tempted to talk upon that line but must not. If you are older than he then try to retrace your steps, remembering your costly experiences, until you come to his level of understanding. He has not lived long enough to appreciate your good advice. He may listen out of respect, but it is most difficult for him to see how in any way, his present condition and mood could be helped by what you are telling him. He cannot feature himself facing results which you suggest. "You cannot put old heads on young shoulders." Use tact and find the *approach* to "where he lives," and work from that angle. Ask God for wisdom to discover the *motive* of appeal, and always remember it is a most delicate and sacred ministry. Drench it with prayer and intense love for his soul and well being.

Let us look again at this lad. The everyday going and coming, the humdrum life of Dad and the home folks nearly kill him. He thinks his brother is perfectly stupid, and all the rest of the world, to him, seems asleep. Oh if he could only *once* do something different, something *he* wanted to do! And what does he *not* think and feel he *could* do!

Perhaps he is still in High School (this is, of course, all imaginary). I have to say this because some people are so unimaginative and literal they would probably ask me for a "proof text" that he ever went to school! Maybe he has finished college and is quite sophisticated, and has acquired that bored air so many young folks have. Life is slow and he has to *endure* so much from the "whole unenlightened universe." Even a college graduate may have a technical knowledge of many points of learning, but there is one thing that a diploma can never give you, and that is the good sense and judgment that come from experience.

Now be patient, you older folk; he is not yet to be blamed. His whole attitude is a part of his nature and outlook. Perhaps he has fought down some foes with which you were never asked to contend. Sometimes people are praised for victory when, after all, it is *not* victory; for the person praised was too great a coward and too weak to be trusted with a real battle. I think we many times look into the eyes of dear souls who bravely meet enemies we are never asked to face. Be tolerant! The lad is not to be condemned, judged, and criticized—he needs help! He needs someone to help *direct* the fire and desire, someone to understandingly assist him, put these fine qualities to use and great blessing. Shall I be frank with you? I like this lad very much. And I like very much every girl and every boy today clothed once more with his temperament and rich possibilities.

I cannot tarry here to consider why he goes to his father, etc. The whole field is fertile, suggestive and real. He can stand the cramping no longer, so he asks of his father his share of goods—"*Give me the portion of goods that falleth to me.*" And here we can find no sin. It was not wrong that he should have what lawfully belonged to him. It was coming to him, and no doubt since he was of age the father consents at once to give him his portion.

Now we come to a field for speculation. It has been a great pleasure for some to let their imagination run on full leash, to sniff all the possible trails of discovery as to *how* he spent, *where* he spent, *why* he spent, and *when* he spent his goods in riotous living. But after all, the detail is not so necessary. At least God thinks so; I am sure He could have told us were it for our good. The point is, he wasted it in riotous living.

Now we find the fault, the sin which brought the younger son to the pigpen. All the different things he did, and the many ways he wasted his substance, are surely wrong. But the chief sin was the *self-will* of inexperienced youth. Self-will is, after all, the root sin of the human race. All the manifestations of sin as we see them in their outworking, are in the last analysis the fruitage of self-will. All this young man did was to have *his own way*. Let that be what it may, it landed him in the place of defeat, failure, tragedy and loss. It always does.

All you have to do to land in hell is to have your

own way in all the thousand patterns it may trace upon
your map of life. The self-will of some men does not
make so ugly a picture, but it will keep them away from
God and truth fully as well as the self-will of another
appearing in more picturesque and colorful trappings. Who
knows but the self-will of the older brother at home may
have been as nasty, in some ways, as that of the younger
brother. At least he did not show a very happy and thankful spirit when his brother returned. I am afraid there
was something "awful good" and perhaps smug about that
older son. I don't seem to feel I would like his general
personality very much. "Awful good" folks bother me
sometimes. Do not mistake me—goodness in itself never
bothers me, for it is like God, and I love God. But *folks'*
goodness does. Do you see the difference?

So now we see our young friend reduced to the level
of a pigpen. He has had, as people say, his fling in
life. He has tried out all the experiments and thrills he
feels he was made for; he has had the tremulous excite-
ment of venturing out upon the thin ice of personal freedom. He has come at last with tired heart and weary
feet to the green hills only to find them decked with the
brush of human experience thousands of years old. All
those wise and subtle suggestions of *his* mind have been
swallowed up in a vortex of human philosophy as old as
the human race. How many, many things he has come to
in his thrilling, bold adventure! He has come to wealth
and he has spent it; to beauty and he has marred it;
to truth and he has ignored it; to life and he has dis-
sipated it.

And now the story says, *he came to himself.* My! my!
What a revelation and what a discovery! Thank God he
met himself. This is the revelation for which he was made.
Only it is sad that he should have to travel so rough a

road, and have to have this auspicious meeting in so un-poetical and crude a place. But never mind the pigpen; it is the place of discovery and revelation for him. Let us think of that and not the pigs. The pen is not the end; it is the first step out and up. Where was *your* pigpen? To what level of the human and sinful failure did you move before you, too, came to yourself? Perhaps your pen had a few straggling morning glories over it to hide its real character, but it takes more than a *morning* glory to hide it. Let us leave the pen. It is *God's* glory that hides us. Thank His wonderful Name!

The youth's restless heart has climbed the hill and now makes friends with him.

Have you, too, come to yourself and sat down to think through to such a revelation? Life (real life) is not a matter of the material world nor to be valued in the com-mon terms used to appraise its worth. Jesus said, *"For a man's life consisteth not in the abundance of the things which he possesseth."* I am glad that He used the word *things.* That is so inclusive, comprehensive and limitless. Material things, of course, come first to mind—money, houses, lands, etc.; but *things* may be otherwise—fame, name, honor, power, intellect, gifts, position, etc. These are also often mistaken for life. So one may have an abundance of these and not have life or know life.

This young man discovers that life consists not in the abundance of things possessed. It is not *things,* but *life,* which is of supreme importance.

Also the lad finds that he is more than the body in which he lives. Man is essentially spirit. The body with all its sensations, acquisitions and functioning is but the vehicle of expression. The invisible, evasive, almost un-known personality is the living reality, and will outlive the poor, perishing body. He came to see these simple, fundamental truths.

There also were the principles and laws of being to be considered, and here the prodigal came upon a field of dynamic truth and power. The temporal, material world is not the world for which he was created. He discovers some of the first, hidden, potential values of character building and spiritual culture. How it thrills him! Pigpen or no pigpen, he cannot remain here. Life means more than things, gifts, or all the material age. So he does the right and only important thing—he goes *home,* confesses his sin and rests at the feet of his father.

I know this story is intensely colorful and dramatic. I want it to be so; and do not let us miss the heart attitudes because of the bodily postures. *"But when he was yet a great way off, his father saw him, and had compassion, and ran, and fell on his neck, and kissed him."* Is that not wonderful? The father does not stand still and wait until the son comes and *falls* at his feet and *begs.* The heart attitude of the Father is never that. He *ran* to meet him. Oh, the deep, unfathomable love of a God like that! God running to meet a sinner, a poor, self-willed fool. How can you keep away from a God like this? I can't half see the robe, the ring and the fatted calf for seeing the anxious, loving heart of the Father. And did he *not* know all the story? Do not worry—He knows only too well.

Now some of you are asking, "What about the prodigal's prayers?" We will come to them soon, but in order to appreciate his prayers let us review a little. What was the character of his first prayer? Was it not, "Give me"? Prayer is a sincere desire of the heart which causes one to focus all his forces toward the realization of that desire. It may not always be expressed in words; it may be the actuating and dominating force in your innermost being causing you to bring to play all your powers for its material gratification.

As a lad at home the younger son was eaten up, as we say, with the desire to hold in his own hands the powers of his life. It became a prayer—*"Give me the portion of goods that falleth to me."* He wanted material things and got them. He misused his powers and gifts in life. He exhausted them, and discovered that they could not and did not serve to satisfy the deep-seated desire for life.

So the revelation of the spiritual side of life and its meaning and the vision of growth and development of the *real* being and personality he found himself to be, roused him to *new* prayer. *"I will arise and go to my father, and will say unto him, Father, I have sinned against heaven and before thee, and am no more worthy to be called thy son:* make me *as one of thy hired servants."* How lofty and glorious such a prayer! Now the father can take a hand in the matter and can *make* him into the desire of his heart.

The Christian character which God desires to manifest through us is not like a gift or an isolated experience which may be realized in a moment. The new birth *is* that and so is the Baptism of the Spirit. Both are spoken of as gifts—and gifts may be received and possessed immediately. But Christian character comes by process, building, growth, and continual development. The new birth is *unto* and the Baptism of the Spirit is unto the eternal purpose of conformity to the divine. Listen to these wonderful words which back up this truth:

"For whom he did foreknow, he also did predestinate to be conformed to *the* image *of his Son."*

"And the glory which thou gavest me I have given them; that they may be one *even as we are one."*

"But we all, with open face, beholding as in a glass the glory of the Lord, are changed into the same image *from glory to glory, even as by the Spirit of the Lord."*

"Beloved, now are we the sons of God, and it doth not yet appear what we shall be: but we know that when he shall appear, we shall be like him; for we shall see him as he is."

"Till we all come in the unity of the faith, and of the knowledge of the Son of God, unto a perfect man, unto the measure of the stature of the fulness of Christ."

We are born of the Spirit and so become partakers of the divine nature which gives us the basic, potential material *for* the ideal. We are also baptized in the Holy Spirit which gives us the *power* for the mighty transformation and accomplishment of His purpose: *making* us witnesses to that image. You will remember Jesus said, *"But ye shall receive power after that the Holy Ghost is come upon you: and ye shall be witness unto me ...."* Note He does not say, "Ye shall become servants unto me." We *serve* by means of gifts and callings, divine and supernatural qualifications. He says, *witnesses*—the word really means *martyr*. It suggests the *whole* life as a living testimony rather than the restricted meaning usually taught—such as to testify, speak, serve or minister for Him. Of course, to testify or speak for Him is included, but is only a fragmentary aspect of this mighty witnessing wrought by the Holy Spirit in the *life* of the believer. The *whole life* witnesses (even unto martyrdom) to His name, character, nature, conduct, likeness and image.

We also receive gifts—gifts of the Spirit. This is the equipment for *service*. We are to occupy until He comes. The gifts thus exercised become channels and means of expression for the life of Christ within.

So you see, my dear, young friends, we are greatly privileged in having in our hearts and working through us the sweet and at the same time powerful Spirit of God. He has come to *make* us. Perhaps you, too, prayed, "Give me, give me," and God gave you the gift of the Spirit (the portion of goods that falleth to you). Is He now *making* you?

Life is primarily for the glory of God. *". . .Whatsoever ye do, do all to the glory of God."* Any spending of life or using of life's gifts or the gifts of the Spirit for selfish or ignoble purposes is wasting your substance in riotous living. You must know there is much riotous living aside from the night-clubs, road-houses, amusement halls and such places. The misuse or abuse of the gifts of life or the Spirit makes riotous living in an Assembly, home or the private life of a Christian. So let us look out and mind our step and don't feel too smug—take a little inventory *now* before you begin to smell a pigpen.

I never saw the possibility of such an experience befalling a Christian until one day in my study the Lord directed me to Paul's letter to the Corinthian Church. Time will not allow me to make a study of this situation and to run, as it were, an analogy between the prodigal son and the Corinthian. Nevertheless, by a few suggestions you may detect it. This church, too, had prayed, "Give me, give me." And God had given her the portion of goods that befell her. She had the testimony that she came behind in no gift. But with all her gifts and power we find her in great need and difficulty until Paul has to write this corrective epistle to her.

What was the matter? The church at Corinth was wasting her substance in riotous living and had not prayed the second prayer, "Make me, make me." The building of Christian character had not kept up with the display of gifts. And that is very possible. We know this from the word Paul uses in the 13th chapter, *"Though I speak with the tongues of men and of angels,"* etc. The word *though* throws the whole matter into possibility. And Paul saw that was just what was the matter. The *motives* back of the use and display of the gifts were wrong. The gifts were right and were of God but the *way* was selfish and not to God's glory. They had power—plenty of power and gifts—but the motive, *love* (born of true Christian character) was missing.

Therefore there were present in the church, unkindness, envy, vaunting, puffed-up spirits, unseemly conduct, provoked spirits, evil surmising, etc., etc., and yet there were gifts and manifestations wonderful to behold. Yes, there was plenty of riotous living and wasting of substance, so Paul *shows* them a better *way*. The thirteenth chapter is the better way, or *law* for the operation of the gifts. They were to have lives backed up by the transforming power of the Spirit. When the church learned to pray the second prayer, "Make me, make me," she became a glorious testimony and witness unto God.

Dear young people, for what are you praying? Are you still wanting things, things, things—even the gifts of the Spirit merely for the sake of having them? Listen, I want you to have gifts, God wants you to have gifts (He even says to pray for them) but with all that, do remember to pray, "Make me, make me." Shall we not all afresh yield our hearts and lives more fully to His wonderful will that He may make us the witnesses He desires in this needy, perishing world?

5.

WHAT DO YOU DO WITH
YOUR SECOND CHOICE?

BELIEVE the Lord has laid on my heart a message of encouragement. So I would like to talk to all those who have problems and difficult matters to settle. While we should all be spiritually minded and inclined, we should be able at the same time to translate that which is of spiritual value into material and worth-while living terms. For if my Christian experience is merely of a theological nature and too theoretical, it does not become workable in my every day life and falls short of much of its purpose. Jesus Christ came not only to die but to teach us *how* to live. I believe He desires to help us translate our problems into opportunities for high living.

I suppose we all have troubles—I hope we do. I like people who have them; people who have blasted hopes, unrealized dreams, tumbled-down air-castles and seemingly wrecked lives. I always feel the possibility of getting somewhere with them. And what a leveler trouble is! It brings us all down to the same place—our common heritage: *"but the Lord delivereth us out of them all."*

Christian workers and evangelists who tell people that when they become Christians life is just one sweet song and a grand picnic misrepresent, I fear, the real life. I must say it is a very peculiar sort of *picnic*. So I hope I may help any who have not walked through the sunny dreams and whose lofty air-castles have no stronger foundations than the cloud they rest upon.

As we read the lives of people we have been impressed by this one fact at least: nearly every one has had to take a second or third choice as far as life's course was concerned. It seems to be an almost universal experience. Very few have moved along smoothly and had their first choice materialize perfectly. They have had to take the fragments and pieces of their first choice in life which has been shattered, mend them together and make a success. Just that has been done over and over again.

When I visited the World's Fair in Chicago, I went to the Art Institute, for I am very fond of pictures and art in any form. I remember I went especially to see Whistler's beautiful picture, his *Mother*. It had been brought from Europe so that America, too, might see this lovely oil.

As I looked at it I saw something more than the picture—I saw the marvel revealed in a *third* choice. Whistler, the world-famous artist, never started out to be an artist. That was far from his thought. Do you know what he started out to be? A soldier at West Point. That does not sound very much like an artist, I am sure. It was his first choice. But while in training at West Point he flunked in his work in chemistry. That was one flunk that God could bless. I sometimes wish a lot of other folks would flunk so they might get started off on the right foot. Whistler then chose engineering and made a grand fizzle of that. Finally he started to paint, with the result that he became a world famous artist, giving to the world some of the very best in painting. His first and second choices crashed but he pieced his hopes together and became the Whistler who is known over the world for his contributions to his field.

Now let me give you an illustration of this truth from

the Scriptures. It is an incident in the life of Paul. It is not recorded merely to give us an item in history but also to teach us a fine spiritual truth. For I believe the Word is Spirit and therefore behind the historic we may find the deeper spiritual teaching waiting for us. I am having a grand time keeping this in mind as I read my Bible. The Word is first spirit, but the truth is very often veiled behind a seemingly insignificant happening.

Let us take the story of Paul as given in the 16th chapter of Acts. Here we find Paul on one of his journeys. He is saved, baptized in the Spirit, and has all the gifts, and is now out in the work. He has a burning zeal for the lost, longing to take the Gospel to the Gentiles, and have churches built here and there over the whole country. It is a godly ambition, wonderful and noble. We read: *"And after they were come to Mysia, they essayed to go into Bithynia, but the Spirit suffered them not. And they passing by Mysia came down to Troas. And a vision appeared to Paul in the night; there stood a man of Macedonia, and prayed him, saying, Come over into Macedonia and help us."*

That is the story for the background for this truth. It reveals one of the methods God uses in dealing with us in building Christian character. Here is Paul, wonderfully gifted, divinely called and commissioned of God, thinking how splendid it would be to go to Bithynia and carry the glad tidings to those who sit in darkness and wait the coming of the Light. Surely there was a great need; and he had the light and the power and the truth. No doubt he thought, "We have the power to communicate this light to those in darkness; let us go at once to Bithynia and save the lost."

It all sounded good. Many things do. It did not sound like the devil, to be sure. It was a fine, noble objective to hold before him. But what did the Lord think about it? He said, "You just keep out of Bithynia." We know it was the Lord, for it reads: *"but the Spirit suffered them not"*; and they *"were forbidden of the Holy Ghost to preach the word in Asia."*

How can you reconcile such a statement? Didn't the Lord love the souls in Bithynia? Certainly. But a missionary call must consist of something more than a consciousness of the need. There were heathen in Bithynia who needed to be converted and Paul had a real burden for them. He could have gone there and established some missions, and swung the entire country. That, no doubt, was very possible, and yet the Lord forbade him to go. How can you reconcile that with what we call our message of today? I don't try to. I don't have to prove the Bible or to explain God. Some people spend half of their lives proving the Bible, keeping God's glory bright, and holding Him on the throne. We were never called to do this. We are called to *live* for Jesus and let God take care of His work.

Here we see Paul, with all the enthusiasm of his heart and burning with a desire to carry the Gospel to the ends of the earth, checked abruptly by God. He *thinks* he has to go to a certain *end* of the earth, but the Lord says, "I want you at another end." And so he, who had such a burden for Bithynia, has to turn around and go down to Troas. Notice that he goes *down*. There is usually a great going *down* after such an experience. But it is God's geography lesson and His road map.

Paul's first choice is ruined. His ambition, though godly and spiritual, is thwarted. Wanting Bithynia but landing in Troas. Did any of you having Bithynia for your objective ever find yourself landing in Troas, a city of which you never dreamed? This is quite a common occurrence and is continually repeated in Christian life and experience.

Paul wanted to go to Bithynia, but he went to Troas instead. Now since he hasn't had his wish fulfilled, do we find him getting into darkness or sitting down to cry over it? No! Paul is patiently waiting till the night season rolls around. Who brought on the night? The Lord. He brings it on out of mercy to create the proper atmosphere. He is getting Paul ready to enter the door that He is about to open. And when it is dark and he knows not which way to turn, Paul realizes his desperate need of the Lord. He can but say, "Lord, you have led me to Troas. What now do you want me to do?"

We see him sitting there, his faith, doubtless, tried to the limit, and all he can see are the towering walls of Troas. So he is wondering what he is to do there. As the shadows of the night gather about him he sees a vision and lo, he hears a voice saying, *"Come over into Macedonia and help us."* That was the field the Lord had for Paul, and we discover something of tremendous importance there. This is the pivot upon which all Christian missions turn. They turn from Asia to Europe and thence to America, and the entire globe is girdled because Paul was obedient; God wanted the Gospel to travel from the East to the West.

What a wonderful day that must have been when Columbus started out from Spain! What a momentous journey that was, for it opened up a brand-new country—just that one little trip of Columbus—and yet what great things hinged on his obedience.

But how much more momentous was the decision which Paul made that day when he said farewell to Bithynia! His hopes were shattered and probably he said, "This is my second choice but since it is God's way I will make this choice to serve me." So he takes hold of the broken bits of his dream for Bithynia, puts them together and starts out to do the will of his Master. And through that obedience he girdles the entire globe. Is it not better to girdle the globe in God's will than to save a few souls in Bithynia?

What was the result of Paul's obedience? He became inseparable from the spread of the Gospel of Christ. We can never think of the great cause of Christianity moving on but that we identify Paul with it. Paul and the great missionary enterprise of that Early Church are inseparably bound together. Isn't it wonderful to think that he dared to let his life be so open to God's will that today Paul is always identified with the missionary enterprise? It was because of the complete surrender of his life.

There have been others who have had their ambitions blasted and have taken of the broken bits and made the second choice to serve them. We have just celebrated another Christmas and many of us have enjoyed the singing of that beautiful hymn which Philips Brooks wrote,

> *"O little town of Bethlehem,*
> *How still we see thee lie."*

I am always glad when they announce that hymn. I can never sing it without thinking of the author, for he was such an instrument in the hands of God for light and truth. He filled a real mission.

But was the ministry Brooks first thought and choice? No, indeed! His Bithynia (first choice) was to be a teacher and he longed to follow that vocation! He finished his college course and then taught school. That was his Bithynia. But he utterly failed as a teacher, broke down, and had to leave. I wish you could read some of the letters he wrote when he was so discouraged and ashamed of himself because he could not make a go of teaching— even though he loved it. He said, "The children are the worst I ever had to deal with." No doubt God permitted them to be unruly; He didn't want Brooks in his Bithynia.

Brooks was obedient to the call of God and landed in his Troas; there he found that the Lord opened a door of great spiritual blessing which would mean much more to the Christian cause than a few village pupils in a schoolhouse. His Bithynia crashed but he took up the broken bits, pieced them together and allowed God to sanctify his life in a fresh channel of spiritual ministry.

How the people loved him! and what a power he was! Among the letters he treasured was one from a cobbler who wrote, "Dear Mr. Brooks: Every time I can I come to hear you preach, because when I hear you preach I forget all about who you are and I find God." Who could want a greater testimony than to have people say when they hear you preach that they forget all about you and find the Lord! He wanted his Bithynia, but he got his Troas.

You who are down in Troas, how are you reacting to your broken dreams, when you find that God has so arranged circumstances in your life as to make it impossible to enter your Bithynia? Can you take a second or a third choice and make it an opportunity in your life? That is a fine test of Christian character. Is your touch with God, and the power of the Holy Spirit in your life strong enough to take that broken first choice and out of it make a splendid chance where God can come in and be glorified afresh? That I am sure, is a challenge to everyone as to the true value of his Christian experience.

Now what did Paul do and how did he gain the victory that he possessed? This *Bithynia* and this *Troas* are of course spiritual states, figurative of the Bithynia of your heart and life and the Troas of your landing.

What did Paul do? First of all, he refused to allow this strange shock to turn him absolutely away from his seemingly prepared channel of expression; he would not allow this movement in life to wreck his faith in God. He would still believe in the supreme and sublime purpose for his life—that he was called of God. If I am yoked up with God then He must have some purpose for me

and I must find my way out of my Troas to be a
channel for God to use me. So Paul says, "Troas, I
shall use you as a means whereby a door shall open
and I shall find my place where God will use me."

It took great faith on the part of Paul to do that.
It took courage not to sit down and let self pity come
in and eat up his faith and joy. Self pity will damn
you quicker than tobacco will. Paul didn't sit down and say,
"if only," "if," "if." Have you noticed that the *ifs* are
always in everyone else but yourself? "If *he* had not
failed," or "If *she* had not said that mean thing." No,
Paul did not develop a case of the *ifs* as some would
have done. That might have blotted God out of the picture.
You can wreck your faith by "if-ing" and by self-pity.

Come now, let us see who is back of all this maneu-
vering. Was it the devil that shut Paul out of Bithynia?
Was it unbelief? Was it sin in his life? No, it was
nothing short of God. So it didn't matter to Paul if all
the people got whispering around and saying, "There must
be something wrong with Paul. He had such a wonderful
opening there and now there is nothing doing. We need
to pray for him"; "Isn't it sad, Paul doesn't seem to be
getting anywhere. I remember when the Spirit was on
him and he had such wonderful gifts and now he can't
even open up a little mission in Bithynia. He is just
sitting down there in Troas. I wonder if the Lord has
cast him off."

Just be patient. Let the night fall heavily upon him,
for it is in the night that one gets a vision and it is in
the night that one hears a voice. How does Paul meet
this situation? He meets it in sublime faith, a faith that
says, "I am walking before God and not trying to walk
before fifty-seven varieties of people; yes, God, You can
carry out Your plan for me." And so Paul walks before

God and stays in Troas while all the saints are wondering what could be the matter with him. I am glad for his courage. There he stays, waiting for the shadows of the night to deepen so he can see the vision and hear the voice.

Have you ever been in Troas? Could you by faith reckon, "My life is dedicated to God? I am intertwined and fastened to this supreme purpose of God and if He sees good to close Bithynia, I know He will open up a Troas sometime, somewhere. I shall wait and be patient." Does the door open immediately for Paul? Perhaps not, but he ties himself up to this supreme will of God, whether it be pleasing to his fancy or not.

Did he stay in Troas? No. It was but a doorway to all the rest of the world; a doorway for the rest of his life. The change was not easy, and yet he became so bound up in the will of God and such a love slave to Jesus Christ that you cannot separate him from it any more than you can separate the name Judson from Burma.

When you think of Judson you always think of Burma and yet Burma was not his first choice. He went to India but the officials would not allow him to stay there. They put him on a boat and after some very painful experiences he finally landed in Burma. He decided that he might just as well be in the will of God in Burma as any other place. Today his name spells Burma. Like Paul of old, he was able to take his broken dreams, piece them together, and in the will of God, with the grace of God, he was able to make it a *finis*.

Can you do that by faith? Can you keep your life surrendered to the special purpose that God has for you?

What does Paul do next? He is obedient to this call that says, *"Come over into Macedonia."* Now, he doesn't know what Macedonia means nor is he enlightened as to its great privileges. He knew that Bithynia was at that time one of the richest countries, a most inviting field; but as for Troas he knew nothing. Did you ever have the Lord close the most inviting field, bar you from the richest opportunities, and put you into a schoolhouse? put you into a corner to labor with four or five people to listen to you? And that, just about as you were to go into Bithynia? Never mind—Bithynia is not for you; it may be your Troas is a schoolhouse. You had better go through and keep the lamps trimmed, the floors clean, the fires tended, and preach the everlasting Gospel to the four or five, for they may prove to be the door that opens up Macedonia for you later on.

In the meantime Paul is willing to live and serve and pour out his life for everyone who comes his way. Can you do that, or will you wait till you can go out with your brief case and preach? Can you serve some other way? It takes more than a brief case and white necktie to make a true servant of the Lord. Can you stand your Troas? Then stay there till the vision shapes itself before you and you hear the voice of the man of Macedonia.

Paul could have felt sorry for himself and so confused over the unkind things the people were saying that he might have developed an ugly spirit toward them. I like these lines of Edwin Markham:

> "He drew a circle that shut me out—
> Heretic, rebel, a thing to flout.
> But Love and I had the wit to win,
> We drew a circle that took him in."

Can you be *big* enough to say, "I will love you in spite of. it; I will make a circle that shuts you in with God and me"? That is being like the Lord. Don't sit down in Troas and *mourn,* but sit through your hour of darkness and listen for the Voice, and as sure as you live, God will open the door which He wants you to enter, where you may serve Him far better than you could have done in Bithynia.

We find the same true even in the life of Jesus Christ. His first great desire was a ministry among His own people, to pour out His heart for His own nation, but *"His own received Him not."* He wanted Israel but that Bithynia never opened to Him. He found Calvary instead— His Troas. What did He do? He made Calvary, made Troas, to become the doorway to Macedonia and to all the ends of the earth.

Dear hearts, take courage! If your life is truly dedicated to God, you need not fear. Let *Him* direct your life. Even though in your *natural* religious life a Bithynia may look most inviting, it may be God's will to turn you to Troas. Wait patiently there, and though the shadows deepen, keep praying.

O Bithynia, it is not for me to enter your fields though they be rich. Troas, here I am. Shelter me in the night that I may rest in your streets. And oh, gentle night, be kind to me. Give me the strength and grace to say "Yes" to the man of Macedonia, for out of the broken fragments of my first choice I shall mend together a most glorious opportunity in which God may rest and delight Himself.

6.

WAITING UPON GOD

"But they that wait upon the Lord shall renew their strength; they shall mount up with wings as eagles; they shall run, and not be weary; and they shall walk, and not faint."—Isaiah 40:31.

THIS is a very familiar promise and one which most of us have delighted to repeat as a comfort and means of strength to our fainting hearts. But do we not find the blessings mentioned here uncommon in our lives? I fear the truth too many times is that we run and *are* weary, we walk and *do* faint.

Let us look at it again—*They that wait upon the Lord* .... Here we find one condition upon which the four resultant blessings hang. This one condition of waiting upon God is entirely within the reach of all, whatever may be the age, condition or environment. God has made it purposely so that all may come into a realization of His blessings. All may not be able to preach, teach, go as missionaries or enter into public service, but any Christian can wait upon the Lord. Here is another word of encouragement. The four promised blessings are backed up by the *shall* of Jehovah God. This gives it power and authority. It is not the word or promise of man with the fulfillment dependent upon his frailty; but the Word of God in heaven and as pure as His name and character. The question then is concerning our part—waiting upon God. This sole condition met, the resultant blessings are sure. Obvi-

ously, then, the absence of the blessing proves that either
we do not meet the condition or we do not understand
its meaning.

We like certain promises of Scripture largely because we
feel there is something strong, beautiful, and triumphant in
them, but we do not really consider what they mean. What
does the Scripture mean by *waiting upon God*? Everything
hinges upon that.

First of all let us rid our minds of one idea common
to all of us—waiting upon the Lord never means praying
or prayer. *To wait,* according to Scripture, *never* means
prayer, in the general sense of petition and asking. This
does not mean that we are not to pray. Prayer has its own
great and unique place in the Christian's life and I only
wish we realized more fully its importance and power, but
prayer is not my theme. As prayer has its distinct place
and part in the Christian's life, so has waiting upon the
Lord its place and meaning. May the Holy Spirit help us
to find a clearer revelation of its meaning, that, having done
our praying, we may know how intelligently and in faith
to wait upon the Lord. Prayer is precedent to waiting.
They are inseparable.

Upon study, I find the Bible tells us much about waiting. It is used seventy-six times in the Old Testament with
twenty-five different phases or degrees of meaning and
twenty-one times in the New Testament with eight different
meanings. These many uses of the word may be divided
and grouped under four general divisions, thus giving the
word four general meanings. I want to consider these four
uses and thus open to our hearts what God means when
He says, to *wait upon the Lord*.

The *first* meaning of the word is *silence*—to be silent.
That does not sound like prayer or intercession does it?
Of course not, for prayer is supposed to have been made

and now the soul is hushed and, bowing in silence (in faith) it waits before God. The heart has been poured out, and now lifted upon the wings of prayer the message is wafted up and away through the silent reaches of space to the Father's throne. And while the Father hears and works, the soul is hushed in silence, waiting. The Psalmist makes use of this meaning of the word in Psa. 62:1, 5.

> *Truly my soul waiteth upon God;*
> *From Him cometh my salvation.*
> *My soul, wait thou only upon God;*
> *For my expectation is from Him.*

It is as if in some great trial or pressure he had found great comfort in prayer and had encouraged his heart in the hope of God's help; then in quiet faith casts himself upon God. This waiting is like a holy benediction, a breath from the life-giving spirit to quiet. It is like the dew of heaven which distills and waters our feverish hearts. We are living in an age of intense activity. The very atmosphere is charged with a spirit of hurry and rush. This spirit influences our spiritual life in too great a measure and works damage to its development. Our souls are too noisy. In prayer life alone see how it hinders. Our hearts are much distressed and burdened, so we go to prayer and maybe spend much time pouring out our petitions before the throne. And too many times we get up immediately, rush out of His presence and often try to answer the prayer by some efforts of our own. We do the praying but not the waiting. Let us not be afraid to be silent before Him thinking it is wasted time. He does not want us to be all the time talking—telling Him so many things about which He already knows more than we do. Time is needed today for proper adjustment to Him, our vision properly focused, our hearts hushed, and minds subdued. This is not all accomplished by prayer. Prayers are needed. They are the winged messengers to carry the need to God. But it is in the silent hour before Him, quietly waiting in His presence that the miracle is wrought.

The *second* meaning of the word carries the thought of *expectation and hope*. Twenty-two times we find this use of the word. To wait upon God means to expect from God. A real "waiting meeting" according to Scripture is an expectation meeting. It implies dependence. How necessary today that we wait upon God in the sense of expecting from Him. The natural man is so self-sufficient. He turns here and there and expects help from his natural ability, from friends or from circumstances. The whole trend of present-day teaching only builds him up in this independence. It has crowded itself into the religious world and today man is taught that he is his own saviour—that he need not expect help from any other but his own being. How contrary to all the teaching of the Word. Quite true that on the natural plane there is occasion for man to help himself and not be dependent. But in the spiritual life we are taught to distrust self and to depend upon the power of the Holy Spirit. As Christians we may have learned this lesson in the initial steps of salvation and may be fully convinced of the need of help from God in that particular. Are we as thoroughly convinced of the absolute need of expecting from Him everything for the maintenance of that new life? Remember the words of Paul, *"For I know that in me (that is, in my flesh) dwelleth no good thing"*—also the words of Christ, *"I can of mine own self do nothing."* Truly *we* need to expect from God. How patient He is in reducing us. He has His own peculiar methods, but if we will submit to His order, He will reduce, crowd and strip us until with the Psalmist of old we cry, "My expectation is from Him."

"Wait on the Lord; be of good courage, and he shall strengthen thine heart: wait I say, on the Lord."—Psalm 27:14.

Here we find David again pressed and almost discouraged. He refused to expect anything from his own efforts but looking away from the frailty of the natural, with triumphant faith he sings out his heart to God, *"All my expectation is from thee."*

The *third* meaning of wait is *to watch, observe, take notice.* This means that all our spiritual senses must be alive, alert and expectant. To wait means that we are to be *near* to Him and *still* that we may catch the slightest intimation on His part. Our hearts are to be sensitive enough to catch the faintest reflection and be able to discern quickly His voice. The meaning is clearly shown in Proverbs 8:34.

"Blessed is the man that heareth me; watching daily at my gates, waiting at the posts of my doors."

"Whoso keepeth the fig tree shall eat the fruit thereof; so he that waiteth on his master shall be honored."—Proverbs 27:18.

Here we have a man, maybe a servant or soldier waiting at a door or gate. He does not know the moment his master may open the door to require his service, or maybe to give him a gift. Be it one or the other it matters not to the waiting man. His duty is to wait (to watch or take notice). It is not the waiting of an idler; it is not the waiting of a dreamer. It is the quiet waiting of one who is girt and ready. We do not long watch or observe keenly the movements of God before He has some word for us. He bids us go or come on some mission, or speak, write, pray, visit, or sing for Him. Why? Because we were near enough to feel what is on His heart, and thus we were able to enter into fellowship with Him in service. Many today do not understand the movement of God in the world as He is speaking to us in present conditions because they are not *near* enough or *still* enough to *observe* Him. As Christians today our faith is not wrecked because of the condi-

tions about us, nor are we deluded and led into world-
wide Church reform movements, because we know what the
conditions mean. We have seen and do see God's hand in
it all and because of a peculiar and holy response in our
hearts we know that God has risen up and that our redemption draweth nigh.

The *fourth* meaning of wait, is *to serve,* or *minister,* and
closely follows the third meaning, to watch. The meaning
is clearly taught in 2 Sam. 23. David had many mighty
men, but three among them were chief.   What special
service made them chief? One day when David was being
hunted, as he said, "like a partridge, on the mountains of
Israel," when he was very far from the throne, and only
faith could see him as King, the garrison of the Philistines
was in Bethlehem, and he longed and said: *"Oh, that one
would give me drink of the water of the well of Bethlehem which is by the gate!"* It was not a command, but
three men heard the wish breathed out of David's heart,
and risking their lives, they broke through the host of Philistines and drew water out of the well by the gate, etc.,
and fought their way back again and brought the water
to David. They were *near* enough and *still* enough to hear
David's sigh, and that sigh was to them a command.

Such wonderful blessings hang upon this one condition—
to wait. Do we wait? Are we silent unto God? Is our expectation from Him or from ourselves, friends or circumstances? Do we watch for His movements that we may
serve?

Shall we gather up the meanings of this word *wait,* and
weave them into a Scriptural definition? To wait upon God
is to have the heart hushed or silent in an *expectant* attitude, to *hear* what He might say that we might *do* His
bidding.

Now let us consider the four resultant blessings which

must follow because God says so. First—*they shall renew their strength*. This is a very expressive term and most helpful. To renew strength really means to exchange strength. It is the same term used when speaking of a change of garments. They shall lay aside their strength, and put on, as a garment, strength from God. How suggestive! How needed this is on the part of Christians today. Many feel that they are strong and may boast of it. And so indeed they are in the sphere of the natural, but it is a strength which utterly breaks down in the sphere of the Christian's life. Our great need is to rid ourselves of self-strength that God may clothe us with His own strength. And that is the first blessing promised to those who wait upon God. Did you ever notice the whole fortieth chapter of Isaiah is a series of contrasts between the frailty and feebleness of man and the strength and greatness of God? *"All flesh is grass—but the word of our God shall endure forever." "It is He that sitteth upon the circle of the earth—and the inhabitants thereof are as grasshoppers."*

While praying over this idea of exchanging strength, I wondered why it should be necessary to exchange so many times. The Lord made me see that it was because of normal growth in the spiritual; just the same as growth in the natural necessitates the changing of garments. Have we not all noticed a young boy—how he outgrows his clothes so soon and sometimes needs to exchange a suit before it is really worn out? It is not a question of the suit being worn or shabby as much as it is a question of growth. So in our Christian development, we need many changes of garments (spiritually speaking). Many experiences, blessings and manifestations, which served beautifully at one time in our Christian development utterly come short now. Owing to a deepening in God and greater room being made in our hearts, the demand comes for more of God, an ex-

change of garments, and a fuller revelation of His Spirit.
It is not a sign that we have out-grown God or worn out
His blessing—that is foolish. It is a sign that as healthy,
normal Christians we are growing and that God desires to
reclothe us with fresh blessings, fresh experiences, fresh
touches and manifestations. He is rich; His wardrobe is full.
Let us trust Him to clothe us anew.

To many this is not an agreeable thought. They think
they must give up or deny some blessing or experience, or
go back upon some of His manifestations which have been
such a comfort and delight. I am sure God does not want
us to deny, forget or belittle any of His blessings; but surely He wants to clothe us with garments convenient and suit-
able to our age and development. If we are now "grown
up sons" or even Fathers and Mothers in Israel, He cannot want us clothed in children's garments. Nor does He
want the young Christian, inexperienced and just coming into the joy of first strength to conform to the dress of an old
saint (spiritually speaking). It would be foolish for the
young Christian to affect the deportment and life of an
old saint when he possesses none of his character. Let
God do the clothing. He has you in hand today making
an exchange of garments. Do you feel that someway you
are being stripped of former joys, and delightful moods?
Are you sensing a dryness in some department of your life?
Is He revolutionizing your prayer life? Maybe in your service you cannot minister in just the same power as formerly.
Does it seem hard to get blessed in *just exactly* the same
way you used to? You are not conscious of any sin or
failure and yet you cannot make things *go* just as you used
to make them move. O, friends, just praise the Lord! It
is a most wholesome sign. You have outgrown your garment and God is wanting to clothe you afresh. Here many
fail because it entails embarrassment to "stand still" so God

can work. They appear back-slidden, dried up or cold to those who have no eyes to see, or to less spiritual members. Many cannot get faith and courage enough to stand, so they do what the growing boy does who is conscious of the smallness of his suit. (Spiritually speaking) they begin to pick and to pull at their sleeves to make them "appear longer," and try to keep the coat (an old experience) snugly buttoned—and it is so uncomfortable. They make a ridiculous spectacle (but sad one) to those who discern the situation. Do not try to stretch an experience or blessing which is not suited to cover you in your present stage of growth. Tell it to the Lord and stand still until He can effect a change. In Psa. 25:5 the word *wait* literally means *stand still*. It is so needed on our part if we are to exchange our strength. Have you ever tried to dress a little child? Mothers know what it means. How many times during the act of dressing, do you have to say, "stand still, stand still"? God has as much trouble with His children when He so desires to clothe us in the beautiful garments of the Spirit.

Now let us consider the second blessing promised. It is but a logical result of waiting upon God and exchanging strength—*they shall mount up with wings as eagles*. I believe the Lord purposely uses the eagle as a type here because of the special peculiarities of that bird. One summer while in Yellowstone National Park, I had occasion to study or observe some eagles in their natural habitat—and thereby learned some helpful lessons. I think He speaks of an eagle because it is the only bird which goes high enough and sustains its position. They have been known to fly at an height of 6,000 feet. The lark also may reach the upper heights and pour out its songs, but it does not stay so long in the heavens. God seats us "together with Christ in heavenly places." That is where He sees us in our new-creation life and where He has called us to live. We are heaven-born and now our affections are on things above. Let us trust the Spirit to hold us in our lofty place. While there, our vision of things is vastly different. We see, as does the eagle, with bird's-eye-view the complex and trying circumstances and conditions and seeing from His side we are able to note the relation of one thing to another. Our hearts are concerned with the whole, the ultimate end rather than isolated or disjointed details and sections. Thus we are able to move on in faith as we look at matters from God's side. If we choose we may look with the limited vision of the natural (our judgment comes into play) and ere we know it we are out of faith. Refuse to look at the situation from the earth side. Let us mount up and let our wings sweep the upper air.

The eagle, I found, had to do with big things—mountains, canyons, great depths and immense heights. The sparrow may be contented to chirp and quarrel in the noisy streets. But in the Grand Canyon—one of the most stupendous and alluring spectacles that nature ever spread out for the wonder and delight of mortal eye—is where I found eagles. There is something so majestic and elevating in the nature of an eagle to choose such surroundings as its native haunt. Truly God has opened to us as Christians a life potent with unmeasured possibilities. The life of a Christian as contrasted with that of the man of the world has to do with the most sublime realities, the most tremendous issues and wonderful destiny. May the Holy Spirit bring us more into a realization of the dignity and wonder of it all. Not to incite pride in the old creation, but humility; that our hearts being subdued and yielded may partake of the nature and character of heavenly and eternal things with which God delights to occupy us. Let God fill our vision with some of the depth, magnitude and mystery of His plan. We would have less time for small talk and non-essentials.

The eagle is not often seen—he is the most solitary of all birds. Many birds are common to sight and even afford amusement. Parrots can talk and entertain, causing remarks and comment. The eagle stays *alone*. Did you ever hear of a flock of eagles! The noisy geese go in flocks. But who wants to be a goose? God seeks eaglemen. No man ever comes into realization of the best things of God, who does not, upon the Godward side of his life, learn to walk *alone* with God. Had we time we could trace through the Word the lives of many of God's eaglemen. We find Abraham alone upon the heights, but Lot (a just man and saved) dwelling in Sodom. Moses, skilled in all the wisdom of Egypt, must go forty years into the wilderness *alone* with God. Paul, who was filled with Greek learning, and had also sat at the feet of Gamaliel, must go into Arabia and learn the desert life with God. Let God isolate us.

In this isolation experience we develop an independence of faith and life so that the soul needs no longer the constant help, prayer, faith or attention of his neighbor. Such assistance and inspiration from the other members are necessary and have their place in the Christian's development, but there comes a time when they act as a direct hindrance to the individual's faith and welfare. God knows how to shape the circumstances in order to give us an isolation experience. We yield to God and He takes us through something, and when it is over, those about us, who are no less loved than before, are no longer depended upon. We realize that He has wrought some change in us and that the wings of our souls have learned to sweep the upper air.

This isolation produces another characteristic mark—quietness. No other bird can keep quiet as long as an eagle. The soul acquires a new grip upon his life and is now moved by God rather than by things seen. He can trust

God to control his spirit in the most vexing circumstances. Often quietness (self-possession), and silence will prove a mightier rebuke than words. We see this majestic calm and quietness so marked in the life of Christ. We also see it in Paul and others who have yielded fully to God. If we mount up with wings as eagles, we shall often grieve the captious, and must count upon some experience of misunderstanding; but we can keep *quiet*. Listen to Paul, *"a very small thing with me that I should be judged of you, or of man's judgment."* We must avoid this. We may nest low enough to be understood by the natural, get under bondage to people, and be approved; but if we take the upper air we must go alone like the eagle.

Now let us consider the remaining two blessings which come in order as a result of waiting and mounting up. *They shall run and not be weary.* That seems like a tremendous come-down; like a strange anti-climax, and also, —*They shall walk and not faint.* This is not an anticlimax but rather the logical result of waiting. Man's order would be to walk, run, and then mount up and thus reach the gradual growth of the Christian in power and strength. But here God is telling us something different. He is showing us the purpose of all that has gone before. The end in view is the practical everyday life to be lived in the power and energy of the Holy Spirit. We go *up there* that we may serve *down here*.

May God teach us by His Spirit the secret of waiting. Then we shall find that unseen hands have clothed us with power and thus our souls will mount up to be alone with God in silent places. Having our strength renewed in flight, we are pleased to walk and run out upon the errands of the Lord. So doing, this everyday life, prosaic, common, and unbeautiful may be made potent with blessing and lived in the power of the Spirit.

IDENTIFICATION

I am a flame born of celestial fire
I bear a name, Insatiable Desire.
I wear in heart an image all divine,
Past human art, not traced by mortal line.
I hear God call to taste His heavenly power:
I give my all to burn life's single hour.
So let me burn through fetters that would bind;
Thus will I learn and freedom will I find.
I shall return to Love's eternal fire,
There shall I burn—a satisfied desire.

—John Wright Follette

7.

THE INSATIABLE DESIRE
OF THE REDEEMED

MAY I offer, along with the poem, *Identification*, a few notes or suggestions for those who wish to share in its message? These thoughts may be scattered and only hint at lines of thought which issue from the larger theme suggested by the title of the poem.

The question of identification—who we are, and why we are thus caught up in an arrangement so divine as the new creation—is not usually considered sufficiently to give a Christian very substantial ground for his thought processes and ventures in faith. His whole life, no doubt, would take on deeper significance and spiritual color had he a clearer vision to follow. If I am not sure what I am, there is endless confusion in life since I fail to reckon or count myself to be the creature God says I am, and make the mistake of thinking I am what I was before I became a partaker of the divine nature. If I fail to know why I am, then my objectives for living probably are quite foreign to God's purpose, or so much less than the ultimate which He has for me that my life is lost in endless technical habits and side processes. All may be very good but they get me nowhere.

To discover a basic fact of one's being and to use that as a premise from which to *live* or *"work out your own*

salvation with fear and trembling" is of paramount value.
Let us remember that man is essentially spirit. People often
confuse themselves with their bodies. My body is not I.
I am more than my body. My body is merely a medium
of expression, the house in which I live this earthly life.
When we recognize even this fact and work from it, ordering
our lives so as to lay the emphasis on spiritual, invisible,
eternal issues where it belongs, we begin to get adjustments
in the new life which are vital and necessary. Bear this
in mind as you read the poem.

I liken my new being to a flame. In Psalm 104:4 we
read that God makes His ministers a flaming fire. In
Deuteronomy 4:24 we read, *"The Lord thy God is a con-
suming fire."* He revealed Himself to Isaiah, Ezekiel, and
John in the midst of fire. Since I am born of God and
thus have become a partaker of His divine nature (2 Peter
1:4), I like to think of myself as a flame of celestial origin
and one with God, for the heavenly fire not only has touched
me but is ministering now in my whole being, making me
daily more and more like Him. As new creatures we are
born from above—born of God, who is fire—and so we
share now in that nature.

By the strange miracle of a spiritual rebirth, the first *I*
that was found in nature has been changed forever into a
new *I*, a new creature or creation in Christ. God sees us
thus, if we are truly born again, and He continually reckons
with us and for us as a new being. All the life in the
spiritual realm is working toward this goal. That is why
we are born of the Spirit—to give us natures which are
perfectly adapted to the new order of life. All the laws
and principles of the spiritual life are made for this. As
new creatures we are fitted for the finest and highest that
heaven can afford. Christ has paid a tremendous price to
make this possible, so we *"beseech you also that ye receive
not the grace of God in vain."*

My name, Insatiable Desire, is rather a character name. That is, it carries the characteristic mood or tenor of the new creation—*insatiable desire*. When we use the term *desire* we find ourselves in a field of very broad horizons. Desire is at the root of all life and conduct, and may be considered the starting point for all natural urges and drives common to the human nature.

We will not here discuss the fundamental urges—though they are God-given and surely to be recognized if we venture very far in the development of character and the building up of a new creation in Christ. Let us merely observe, in passing, that all the basic urges and hungers in life are according to God's creative scheme and belong to the plan for human life. Through sin and failure they may lose all sense of relation and proportion, and be abused, misused and misdirected. But the wonderful Christ who knows and understands us perfectly can take a poor, distracted personality and cleanse it of sin, fill it with His own powerful and beautiful life, and cause an integration of all the essential elements of our makeup. He centers them upon His own supreme being and builds us anew. He does not destroy; rather, He cleanses and unifies the personality, and causes it to function normally and perfectly for God's glory.

The question of desire has long been debated, and in many lines of philosophic thought it has become a problem. All are conscious of the human urges. Though these urges take various forms, expressions and tones of emphasis, they remain with us. Back of all the forms of outer expression we find desire, for without this they are meaningless. This unique quality in our makeup is God-given and is one of the marks which lifts man above the animal kingdom.

It is not possible for us to do all the things we would like to do, nor to become all that we would like to be, but God sees our desire if it is there. Remember what Paul wrote in 2 Corinthians 8:12 concerning giving: *"If there be first a willing mind* [desire], *it is accepted according to that a man hath, and not according to that he hath not."* It is in the field of desire that God sees us, and it is here that He longs to work with us and help us. But man is so used to the external, tangible world in conduct that often he completely fails because he does not deal directly with the desire question. He gets into conflict, failure or frustration in his outer life because he ignores or is ignorant of the fact that outer conduct is but a reflection of the real man inside.

Most religions have something to say and do with this question, since it is common to all mankind. Hinduism would get rid of it by a process and technique designed to bring the personality to a desireless Brahman. Buddhism offers a different solution—strike it with death and kill all desire for life (a strange and subtle delusion) and so enter Nirvana. But Jesus has the true solution. He recognizes desire as a very necessary part of life, not only on the natural plane but also in the realm of our spirits, and instead of condemning it He creates a new place where it may find release and movement.

Jesus came not to destroy life or desire, neither to deny it nor suppress it. He came to give life and that more abundantly. He elevates this element to a new plane of living, and intensifies it. He comes into our hearts and lives to correct and create by His radiant presence. He sets new objectives before us; He cleanses our desires and adjusts them until we can say with the Psalmist, *"Lord, all my desire is before Thee."* The desires He creates in the heart are for spiritual, eternal qualities rather than material things. Therefore, while we tarry here the hunger and thirst are insatiable. The desire for God becomes an obsession—holy and mystical. The new man hungers and longs for completion. He longs to find adequate fields for expression of hidden, spiritual awakenings and discoveries in this new life.

At the new birth the spiritual man, in a sense, is like a newborn babe. He has within him a holy urge to attain full spiritual development. No doubt this phase of the Christian life was in the mind of Jesus when He said, *"Be ye therefore perfect, even as your Father which is in heaven is perfect"* (*Matthew* 5:48). Do you remember when He spoke those words, and under what conditions? If you do not keep the context in mind you may give them a very different meaning from that which is intended. The word *perfect* that is used here means to complete, or to reach a goal—to be fully grown; to be of full age; to be fully developed in mental and moral character; etc. In Greek it is *teleios*. It appears in Ephesians 4:13; Colossians 1:28; Colossians 4:12; etc. It has reference to something being brought to its maturity, as shown by the rendering of Colossians 4:12—*"That ye may stand perfect and complete in all the will of God."*

When Jesus spoke these words He had just finished one part of the Sermon on the Mount. He had painted a vivid picture of the ideal Christian life. The standard would seem quite impossible for a poor, natural man ever to reach, but Jesus was setting this standard for the new man, not the natural man. He has come to produce that new spiritual man in the believer. All the character qualities He shows in this ideal picture are to be found in the new creation. Jesus paints the picture; then He turns to His disciples and says, in effect: "Here is the ideal and perfect concept of the new man. Here also is the dynamic or the power for making it a reality—the Holy Spirit. I have given you life. I have begun the new creation in your hearts and lives. Now *become completed* and finish the new order."

He is not telling them to go and do something. He wants

them to *become* something. It is easier to do than to be. He presents the blueprint and then tells them to carry it out to completion in their lives. His words were both a challenge and a command. He was not telling them (in the Sermon on the Mount) to be perfect in the sense of being holy and sinless. Nevertheless, the Bible does command us to be holy. See 1 Peter 1:16; 1 Peter 2:9; Ephesians 1:4; 1 Corinthians 7:34, etc. The word used here is *hagios,* meaning sacred, or morally blameless. We are told to be holy. We are also told to go on to perfection (*teleios*); that is, to completeness, to the consummation, to the fulfillment of God's purpose for the new man. We are to *grow.* This is the end toward which God is working. Read Romans 8:29. The Word does not say that God has predestinated us to go to heaven. It does say that He has predestinated us to be conformed to the image of His Son.

Now let us go back to our theme of desire. Desire rules. Jesus recognized this and therefore He demanded a surrender of life in all of its meanings to Himself. We submit our lives to Him in a full surrender, even unto death. This death is the very means by which He releases us from all the hidden dangers that still lurk in the realm of natural life. We reckon ourselves to be dead indeed unto sin, and this very necessary act brings desire up and out upon a spiritual level where it can move freely in God. It becomes sane, safe, holy and amazing in its outreaches. Here nothing upon earth can ever satisfy it. The desire while we tarry here is insatiable; He wants it so. He and He alone is the answer, the center, the source to which the hungry heart ever looks for satisfaction. O matchless Christ! The One solitary grandeur of the world!

"I wear in heart an image all divine." This refers, of course, to the creative act of God. We are created in the image and likeness of God—not a corporeal likeness, but a moral and spiritual likeness, as mentioned in Ephesians 4:23, 24 and Colossians 3:10. The process going on now in the new creation is the restoration of the image of the Son, and our conforming thereto.

"I hear God call to taste His heavenly power." Paul says that we are called *unto a fellowship* (1 Corinthians 1:9). As a rule, people think of God's call as merely a call to heaven, but here we find a call to a fellowship which precedes heaven. This fellowship is a phase of life right here and now on earth, and is for a specific and necessary reason. It is a relationship established by God and it deepens and comes into maturity as one yields to the demands and requirements laid down for its realization. It reaches past the external life of sense.

Many hear God call them from sin and from the world, but I am not now speaking of that call. I speak of a call that comes more definitely to the Christian after the initial steps of salvation, of water baptism, and of Baptism with the Spirit. It reaches the ocean floor of the heart— the seat of desire and motives and the veiled recesses of selfhood. This call reaches the more subtle form of the ego. It gets at the real person. God longs to bring the soul into a conscious relationship with Himself as *fire*. Fire does so many things—it cleanses, frees, reduces, refines. The fire is heavenly and must be so, since no natural force or process planned by man can accomplish the necessary miracle. It demands *all* of life.

"I give my all to burn life's single hour." When I think of the eternal ages ahead and know I am born for them, then this earthly life seems but a single little hour. Oh, but what an important hour! Here and now I must settle and plan the issues which project themselves on into eternity. Christ knew that, and in His teaching concerning the deeper and fuller life, He let His followers know it was no easy matter. He did not say, "Now just confess your sins and accept Christ and all things are yours." Instead He made very stringent and searching demands of those who wish to enter fully into all that He has for us. We must deny ourselves, take up our cross daily, and follow Him (Luke 9:23). Instead of loving our life we must lose it for His sake (Matthew 10:39). We must love Him more than we love our father and mother, wife and children, brothers and sisters (Luke 14:26).

And why? one may ask. Oh, friends, a miracle awaits the one who thus dares to yield all to God. "So let me burn through fetters that would bind." The fire frees and releases the soul. One finds freedom from earthly bondage and the soul experiences a rich spiritual illumination. The fetters of tradition, old forms, religious habits (religious but not born of the Spirit), unscriptural dogmatism and so much of natural setup in the religious life, are burned off. All this and more is consumed in the fire of God.

This flame is like the Word of God—the lovely Truth which now has a ministry in the inner life. As surely as the Blood cleanses us from sin, so does the Truth, this heavenly Fire, cleanse and set free the soul from hindering and binding things which could keep us from entering into that fuller understanding of His glorious purpose for us. "Thus will I learn and freedom will I find." This is the true liberty which God has for those who will pay the price. The Christian life is a series of crises and cycles of growth.

There is a deep and glorious spiritual evolution for those who meet the demands God requires. The new life becomes a schooling and a divine process of becoming. Here we are disentangled and extricated from the old, Adamic setup. Life becomes a series of divinely planned experiences in which God is faithfully working to release us and adjust us to a life in Himself.

How our hearts thrill at the thought of the ultimate victory. For this all creation is waiting and toward it all creation is moving. The heart once set on fire and illuminated in this fellowship can never, never rest in any form or pattern of earthly life. An insatiable desire, a divine discontent, a heavenly restlessness is its holy obsession. Here and now we may give birth to (but not fully realize) the character qualities we desire to possess in the ages to come. We find all these noble and ideal qualities in Christ. He is the embodiment of all perfection, the personification of all truth.

Oh, marvelous and wonderful Christ, we adore and love Him! We are changed as we behold Him. All that our souls desire is found in Him. Our deepest desires shall yet be realized for,

> "I shall return to Love's eternal fire,
>   There shall I burn—a satisfied desire."

We shall return! We are homeward bound! Again, again this restless heart shall melt and move in God. We shall not lose our identity or personality. Each unique personality will persist through the ages. But we shall find a oneness such as Christ prayed for. His prayer shall yet be answered. We shall find in Him that completion for which we were given a new birth.

Yes, we shall continue to burn, glow, and move in God —a satisfied desire!

THE SACRAMENT OF THE HILLS

I have seen beauty my heart cannot sing!
How can I tell in words the sacrament
Of truth God spreads upon the autumn hills?
How strange the silence deep within my breast
When I behold this miracle of grace!
The wine is mighty—drink deeply, my soul,
And taste the dregs of beauty that convict.
My heart, so long athirst for truth and light,
Drink of this wine and know its subtle tang.
O hungry eyes within, look and behold
The glory and the mystery of truth
Eternal and sublime upon the hills.
God's finger traces there in language sure
The message of His strength and endless love.
Beauty translates it and I understand.
A feast is spread—my hungry heart must feed!
The broken bread of glory sacrificed,
Strong meat for thee, O heart of mine, is here.
How can I sing? My heart convicted stands.
O Beauty, how you challenge me to prayer!
Upon my spirit etch thy image fair.
And sing, O heart, this likeness all divine,
Interpret then in life this sacrament
Of truth—the beauty of the autumn hills.

—John Wright Follette

8

POOLS OF HESHBON—HIS REFLECTORS

THIS evening I would like to share with you a little word which has been a comfort and also a means of inspiration to me. One of the precious things about the ministry of the Holy Spirit is that while we are occupied with our daily duties and hungry for a deeper fellowship with our Lord, He is able to whisper to us and draw our attention to some thought in the Word, of which we have been hitherto unconscious.

As consecrated Christians there is something I am sure we share together—a deep desire to please our blessed Lord. The revelation brought to us of possibilities in the realm of the Spirit and degrees of fellowship sometimes overwhelms us. This is due to a consciousness of our limitations and our unlikeness to Him. The ideal is ever there before us and with the *inner man* we desire its realization. But before we know it we become occupied with natural limitations; our faith weakens and we feel very far short of our objective.

Another thing which helps to weaken the personal relation to God and hinders His working in our hearts is to compare our hearts and lives with those of other Christians. This is ruinous and really unscriptural. 2 Cor. 10:12: *"For we dare not make ourselves of the number, or compare ourselves with some that commend themselves, but they measuring themselves by themselves, and comparing themselves among themselves, are not wise."*

One reads or hears of the mighty or spectacular doings

of such and such a brother or sister and he wonders at the display of power and glory. A certain evangelist is a "flame of fire" and hundreds are swept into the kingdom through his ministry. Then we hear of a teacher who opens the Word in a marvelous way and many Christians are deepened in the things of the Lord. Next there is a missionary opening up fresh fields to the Gospel in mighty fashion. And here is a pastor feeding and building up his flock until it becomes phenomenal. And so if one *compares,* as the Bible says, he is soon snowed under amid the storm of wonderings, doubts and questions which blow across his little horizon; and he feels he is just nowhere. And yet all the time he is enjoying sweet fellowship with the Lord and is not conscious of any cloud between; he is not self-seeking nor is he self-willed. But as he reads of the doings of the "mighty men of faith" he feels more than ever out of the game. Then if he is not careful he will do what the children of Egypt did when they saw the children of Israel pass through the sea—they tried it too, and "assaying to do were drowned." Never try to be Paul or Moody or Finney or anybody else. Please be yourself. An attempt at anything else is extremely ridiculous.

This message is "from the abundance of my heart." It is very personal but since we are all of the household of faith and of one family I will share it with you. May you, too, be helped as it helped me. I used to wonder *where* I was in the great plan and *what* I was to do to please my Lord. He had redeemed me and given me a very wonderful baptism in the Holy Spirit, and had called me to a life of peculiar separation unto Himself. Of this I was, and still am, very conscious. I, too, had heard of others being wonderfully used in His service and of some going as missionaries. It was while walking under a cloud of such reports and wonderings in my mind that the Holy

Spirit began to deal with me. Knowing that I was not a flaming evangelist and that I was not called to take up a pastorate and that God had checked my going as a missionary, I felt there was little left for me to do. But I kept yielded and in my heart and will surrendered to the Lord. That does not mean I did not have a thousand thoughts. My heart was restless at times and I did not want to lose time in moving on into the things I knew were possible for a yielded heart.

While in that mood the Holy Spirit kept whispering to me, "Pools of Heshbon. Pools of Heshbon!" And there came a sense of quiet and rest. As soon as my heart began to grow restless I was conscious of His presence and again the whispering of the Spirit in my heart, "Pools of Heshbon! Pools of Heshbon!" I was not sure where the words were in the Bible, being new in the way and not knowing much about the Word, but I found them in the Song of Solomon 7:4, *"Thine eyes (are) like the fishpools in Heshbon,"* etc. In the Song of Solomon we have a very graphic description of the love affair between the Bridegroom and the bride and this is one of the most spiritual bits of Scripture we have. It is the Lord dealing with a heart that has been separated from the world and dedicated unto Himself, a heart that has been wooed and won by the power of the love of God until it stands separated from the world and from itself, and is espoused unto this Bridegroom.

As I read that phrase, *Thine eyes like the fishpools of Heshbon,* I wondered, "What is the Lord saying to me?" And to think it should come just when my heart was distressed and fearful lest it might not bring forth the desired manifestation of His power and grace and beauty which is so evident in other lives! It was just when my heart felt its limitations that the Lord brought to me this picture of the Bridegroom dealing with his bride. Then it was that the Spirit opened to me the meaning of the text as I am giving it in this message.

Let us look at this picture. He is talking about her eyes. The bride is described here from the top of her head to the soles of her feet with every part of her anatomy reflecting some desirable characteristic of beauty. What are the eyes of the bride? What are the eyes of my experience? Eyes always signify intelligence, a seeing power, a discerning power, a beholding power. Many times they mean the power of perception. The eyes are the windows of the soul and often much of the inner life of a person is portrayed in the look of his or her eyes. I might hold up my hand or my foot but it would not tell half as much as when you look me straight in the eyes. I do not like people who can not look me straight in the eyes; I always feel there is something radically wrong somewhere with them.

The Lord delights to look at us right in the eyes—He says so. Sometimes it is much easier to hold up folded hands before Him but He looks right through the folded hands and into our eyes—the eyes of our heart. Have you ever felt that you did not want Him to look you straight in the eyes? His penetrating and sometimes searching look is melting. Oh, the look of those eyes! What penetrating, convincing power! What pleasing, quieting, assuring, and understanding in His eyes! I am sure all He had to do many times was just to look at a person and that would mean more than a thousand words. You know what I mean, I am sure, for have we all not had Him look at us?

So we find that the eye is the symbol of the window or the outlook of the soul; that which portrays our intelligence, our conception. It is the spiritual part of our being without shadow or blur. Open the eyes of your spirit to Him. Do you remember anyone who gave us a little word about this? To the Ephesians Paul says that ever since he had heard of them and their faith he had not failed to pray for them. For what did he pray? *"That the God of our Lord Jesus Christ, the Father of glory, may give unto you the Spirit of wisdom and revelation in the knowledge of him: The eyes of your understanding being enlightened; that ye may know what is the hope of his calling and what the riches of the glory of his inheritance in the saints"* (*Eph.* 1:17, 18).

That is exactly in harmony with the reference concerning the Pools of Heshbon. The eyes are likened unto the deep places—the eye of the soul, the eye of the inner being. Paul was praying that their eyes might be opened and that they might behold the glorious revelations, the wisdom and knowledge hidden away in this wonderful Lord and Master.

Have you ever made a study of the prayers of Paul? In doing so I am sure you will be surprised to find the general burden of them to be different from what we might think. He does not ask God to bless the groups whom He has taken out of the world for His name and in all the services and undertakings in which they might be interested. No, his prayers always center about the question of their growth and development and understanding in the things of God. *"For this cause we also, since the day we heard it, do not cease to pray for you, and to desire that ye might be filled with the knowledge of his will in all wisdom and spiritual understanding; that ye might walk worthy of the Lord unto all pleasing, being fruitful in every good work and increasing in the knowledge of God; strengthened with all might, according to his glorious power, unto all patience and long-suffering with joyfulness"* (*Cor.* 1:9-11). And so in Ephesians 3:14-19, Galatians 4:19, etc.

His great desire is that they might *behold*. He wanted their eyes to be opened. What do they see when they do look? Doctrines? Philosophies? Creeds? Theology? Not these at all. They are to behold *wisdom* and *knowledge in Christ Jesus*. So He becomes the center, the objective towards which their vision is cast. "While we look not at the things seen but at the things not seen." How can you look at something you cannot see? Oh, I see many things which are invisible! And I am finding more and more how very possible it is to behold the things invisible till they become more real than the visible. Look up! Look up! Look up into the eyes of the Beloved.

Why does He say the eyes of the consecrated are like pools? You know water, as an element, is a very wonderful item in the universe. We are mute as we try to think of it in its boundless reaches as manifested in the ocean. But our text does not say, "Thine eyes are like the rolling, tossing sea." And yet how magnificent the sea is! Think of its ministry—binding together the various continents. It is the power of the ocean to touch each shore and to have kingdom fellowship with every portion of the world. It is a great ministry the ocean has—to touch the ends of the earth. Upon its heaving breast the mighty steamers ply their way from one corner of the globe to another. It is the ocean which makes this possible. Yes, the ocean may lift its tossing waves and serve in a marvelous ministry that touches the ends of the earth—but He does not say, "Thine eyes are like the ocean."

Look at the rivers which, in their definite locations hidden away in the hills and mountains, find their courses and come rushing down till finally they reach the sea. The rivers nourish the land, they bring vegetation and life to all the countryside. Upon them the steamers sail and they become arteries of life, of navigation and are a blessing to all the inhabitants where they thread their graceful ways. But He does not say, "Thine eyes are like a river."

Then think of the beautiful waterfalls, the cascades that come rushing down hundreds of feet over the rocks in wondrous beauty. I have so many times gazed on Yosemite Falls and have never tired of its beauty and grandeur. There a stream tumbles down 1,600 feet from a sheer cliff, way, way up in the granite rock. It pours down a thousand, six hundred feet without any interruption at all, a height equal to nine Niagara Falls piled one on top of the other (though not equal in volume). There it comes dashing down the edge of the mighty cliff to a great, foaming basin; then off the edge of that rocky ledge it makes a six-hundred-foot cascade and then one grand leap of four hundred feet to the floor of the valley below. What a gorgeous display it is! The wind gets into it sometimes and blows it all around, giving the appearance of a great, beautiful lace veil. Think of it; a thousand, six hundred feet of lace! God's lace that no man can imitate or make; beautiful patterns that nobody can duplicate. That is just one of God's beautiful displays of water in motion. There are thousands of others, showing His marvelous creative work, wonderful to behold. The face of nature is ever a source of wonder and inspiration to me. I love her in all moods and at all seasons. Nature is the inarticulate voice of our Father speaking to us; the first, primitive, simple revelation of God to all people who are supposed to discern Him back of the manifestation. So I am a lover of the primitive and elemental things. I enjoy the simplicity and beauty of their power. I like to feel my relation to them—I am of the dust and I am very conscious of it. Well, that was a waterfall spectacular and wonderful! But he does not say, "Thine eyes are like the waterfall. " What does He say? He looks down at our broken hearts washed in His precious blood, now dedicated to Him and filled with His love and Spirit and He says, *"Thine eyes are like the pools of Heshbon."*

How does the pool differ from the ocean? the river? the

waterfall? Where did the pool come from? Oh, dear ones
He *dug* the pool; He dug it deep in our lives. Whence
came my pool? Way down, in the inner, hidden parts of
my life and nature, the penetrating power of God dug deep,
deep, DEEP. It makes me think of my boyhood days spent
on a farm and the old well on it which my ancestors dug
more than a century ago. They dug deep into the side of
the hill with hard, laborious work; and then they carried
stones, firm and strong, from the fence-rows and fields. Then
somebody went down into the well and laid it all about
with stones, packed and fitted them into the sides and walls
of the well, stone by stone, clear to the top. At the bottom
was a spring which flowed freely until the well was filled
with clean, cool water—the best I think I ever tasted.

Listen! He is saying, *"Thine eyes are like the pools of
Heshbon."* He saw the possibilities of making in your heart
and in mine a beautiful, deep pool. *Who* made it? The
Lord, dear soul, the Lord. Did you never hear Him digging
in the deeper places of your life? Until you have said,
"But Lord, this is so hard. Why do You have to dig so
deep?" Do you wonder now at the severe measures of His
discipline? Do you still question the loving demands He
made when you laid down your heart and life at His feet?
*"Think it not strange concerning the fiery trial which is to
try you...."* Have you not yet learned to love the blow
that sets you free? I like so very much what Robert
Browning said,

> *"Then welcome each rebuff*
> *That turns earth's smoothness rough,*
> *Each sting that bids nor sit nor stand but go!*
> *Be our joys three-part pain!*
> *Strive, and hold cheap the strain;*
> *Learn, nor account the pang; dare,*
> *Never grudge the throe."*

Such are the experiences of a loving, dedicated heart. Then it is that we hear the thud, thud, thud, of the power of God digging down to the very roots of our being. But it is only there that He can release the springs of water bubbling, gurgling and gushing up with eternal freshness. He did not *pour* the water into the pool. It came bubbling up from hidden springs. And then lest the mud and slime of the natural (the old creation) might pollute the water He lined the pool with the stones of truth. These He dug from the quarry of His Word. He brings these heavy stones of truth and packs them all around the sides of the pool. Has He not sometimes brought you a truth which seemed very hard and heavy, and before you had it properly placed it seemed He brought another? Do not worry. He brought them that the precious water of life might not be polluted by human touch.

Then He comes near—oh, so very near, and stands so still by the side of the pool! As I was conscious of His presence and did not hear His voice I wondered *why* my heart was so quiet and hushed? The Holy Spirit kept saying, "Pools of Heshbon! Pools of Heshbon!" And like a revelation He flashed this word across my heart—"The charm of the pool is its power to reflect." The vast ocean roaring with its might and reaching out its great heaving tides is too boisterous to reflect. The river, turbulent and muddy, sweeping onward, ever onward, is never still enough. It is too busy to reflect. It has great burdens to bear and ships to float and so cannot tarry. And alas! the dashing, crashing, thundering waterfall is hopeless as far as ever gathering up its waters into a quiet pool is concerned. Not even a stately tree is reflected in it. The Bridegroom is not looking for the ocean. He does not tarry long in the presence of a spectacular waterfall, nor does He linger by the rapidly flowing river. He does come, thank God, by the side of a quiet pool, which He has dug deep in the very nature and life of one who loves Him and has dared to let Him work there.

Oh, the mystery and beauty of such a fellowship! Is it not most humbling to any pride of the human? Have we one thing of which we can boast? Nothing! Only a pool of limpid, clean, quiet water. Yes, water, that weak element—even a by-word among men, "weak as water." Blessed weakness! *"For ye see your calling, brethren, how that not many wise men after the flesh, not many mighty, not many noble, are called: but God hath chosen the foolish things of the world to confound the wise; and God hath chosen the weak things of the world to confound the things that are mighty; and base things of the world, and things which are despised, hath God chosen, yea, and things which are not, to bring to naught things that are: that no flesh should glory in his presence"* (*I Cor.* 1:26-28).

Can you not be a pool, dear heart, for God? The pool in itself has no strength but it can reflect a whole range of mountains. The lofty mountains of His strength are in our hearts when we let them reflect there. We cannot produce them; we only reflect them. He is made unto me all I need—wisdom, righteousness, power and all else. The sky—His sky of eternal blue and of heavenly character—is over me. My sky is dull and very limited, but I can reflect *His* sky. Only a pool—not destined to traverse the road-ways of the world, but called to a commonplace and uneventful life. Yet when turned to Him it may reflect the very passions and burdens of His loving heart. I hear someone say,

"My life is so full of shadows and at times I am called upon to count the lonely vigils of the night."

Yes, I know. There are others who have known the glory of the sun in noonday splendor. Now they have seen it set beyond the distant hills. The glory of the past, now a haunting memory, would still lighten up the deep twilight like a friendly afterglow. Yes, yes, dear souls! But listen! I asked about the night saints, those who are called to tarry and know the language of the night watches. Though the shadows darken and the night be dark—look for one little token of His love—a star. What could be more thrilling than to behold in the deep, dark blue—the unspeakable deep of midnight, a point, a luminous, brillant twinkling point of light—a star? That is His promise of hope. It is there. Yes, it is there. Oh, the power it has to transport the heart! One becomes detached from material things and the here and now.

It is the distant point in the eternal bosom of the Father, to which my redeemed soul is journeying. It is the point of the mystical union of my soul with that of my heavenly Bridegroom, the sequel for which all this *process of becoming* is intended. A star! I cannot create one. I cannot fathom the meaning of its message and the story of my destiny but I can *reflect* one. I have no mountains of strength, no heavenly sky, no pageantry of sunset, no star of hope. I can produce none of these. I am but a pool of limpid, weak, clean water within the embrace of these stones of truth packed down in the innermost parts of my being. But the strength of His character, the purity of His heavens, the glory which is only His, and the Hope which He Himself is, may all be *reflected* in my pool, even my heart.

Dear one, do you want to please Him? May I encourage you? He has many oceans, countless rivers, and innumerable waterfalls, but so few pools. Pools are *costly*. You might as well learn that now as later. He digs them Himself, but only in loving, yielded hearts. Do not try to make one! He longs that there be a fresh revelation (by way of reflection) of His power, beauty and character to the needy world. Do not grieve if you are not one of the other water manifestations. He may want a Pool of Heshbon in your heart. Let Him dig. And oh, He will fill it (from *hidden* springs) sweet, clean and refreshing. Let Him work. And *please* be still while He deals with you. It saves a lot of time. To let Him line your inner life with the hard, heavy stones of truth from His quarry will stand you in good stead.

Yes, there is the temptation to be any or all of the other water displays, but remember, *none* of them *reflect.* There were NO eyes in them for Him. He wants to look into the eyes and be satisfied. Only to know He has looked into the eyes of the soul as it stands before Him (alone and unafraid) to hear Him say gently, "Pools of Heshbon!" is not to be compared with any earthly experience. It is divine, celestial and spiritual. Let Him dig down, down, into the deep, hidden places of your life. Let Him make room in the heart and He will fill it. Let there be one more Pool of Heshbon for the Bridegroom of the soul.

9.

THE PURPOSE OF ADAM'S TEST

N 1 Peter 2:2 we find a very suggestive statement or command, *"As new born babes desire the sincere milk of the word, that ye may grow thereby."* Some people seem to think it reads, "That ye may be happy thereby," or "That ye may be refreshed." One might be both happy and refreshed in reading the Word; but the ultimate and final purpose of all real Bible study is given here, *That ye may grow thereby.* It is the reaction upon the spirit of the man that counts.

What effect or power has the Word upon your life? Do you continue to be just the same in spiritual measure, or do you find there is a mighty and mystical power moving in your inner being when the *Word is mixed with faith,* which causes you to grow? I do not want to discourage anyone from Bible study—we need to know our Bible better. But even in this department of our Christian life there lurks a danger, *"For the letter killeth, but the Spirit giveth life."* One may know the letter of the Word and its prophecies and be able to teach and preach and handle the Word wonderfully, from an intellectual point, and yet quite fail of the purpose God has in giving revelation. Unless one has the Spirit who breathed the Word, to interpret and quicken it to the inner life, there can be no growth spiritually. There may be amazing growth in mind and interest but these alone are not what God is after. So there is danger in knowing the scriptural settings of many of the doctrinal subjects which hold the attention of Christians and yet failing to have the power and spiritual significance of the same wrought out and reflected in the life and conduct of the one who *knows* all about the matter.

I think just now of the truth of the Second Coming—one of the choice teachings today. What a Blessed Hope! We could not fit in with any program of man and would be absolutely at sea did we not cherish this Hope and have the strength of its courage to back us. But why know all the technical prophecies and verses and their hair-splitting issues; why be able to chart the course of all nations and peoples, and not be ready when He comes! It is like studying a timetable and being able to name all the stations (in their order) and give the mileage, give descriptions of the country, and population of the cities, and alas! not have your ticket! I would rather read slowly and digest the Word than to read much and not have it made alive. We sit 'neath a blaze of light these days—how much *light* has been converted into Life? Let us keep balanced. We do not discourage the study of the Word, but let us trust His Spirit to quicken it to us and let it have power to cause us to grow.

We read in John 8:32, *"And ye shall know the truth, and the truth shall make you free."* Here a suggestion of the purpose of study is given us. It shall set us free. Do not limit that to sin or to the apparent failures where we need the power of His redemption to liberate us. Truth is universal and absolute. No one has a corner on it. It is most powerful. It frees us from all bindings of the old creation, its teachings, philosophies and earthborn visions. As truth enters it frees us from mental and traditional hangovers of the old life. We need its continual liberating power. Why? *"That we may grow thereby."*

The new creation of Christ-life *feeds* upon the Spirit of truth. The revelation dawns and we are conscious that we are in a new realm. The mighty salvation, the glorious Baptism, the call of God, the thrusting out into service— all are wonderful and of God. But not one of them in itself can mature a soul. None are given because they can mature one—they are given because we are immature and need to grow. How many disappointed people there are! Do not mistake me. Not that they are disappointed in a very real and moving experience, but so many have found that the experience, in itself, did not do what they had expected. They had wonderful and marvelous experiences, yet after being in the way a while, they found they had to grow and be subject to a "process of becoming" and a life of discipline and training if ever they hoped to realize in actual life the vision of possibility held out in the experiences themselves. All experiences, services rendered, manifestation of His life in us are to an end—transformation, conforming, growth, building, edification, perfecting. So do not "park" on any one of the highways of the divine plan. Keep your vision up where it belongs. Let your thought life in these matters hold correct perspective and keep your emphasis on the things the Word has it on. Study and desire and hunger for the truth that you may grow and come into the purposes of God for you.

This matter of *growth* brings to mind the thought of God in our first parents. For a little study let us turn to the account of creation as given in Genesis. Here we find that God creates man. The Hebrew word, *bara*, suggests a specific act, not a process, not an evolving and coming from a lower order. In the act of creation man became a partaker of human nature. That is, he was created by God a human being—he possessed the natural, human make-up. In the Word we find there are four natures mentioned—the divine, angelic, human, and animal. These are each a special and specific order or form.

God is characterized by the divine nature—there are certain attributes, but we cannot go into detail concerning them. Enough to say, He is bound, limited as God, the Absolute, by the nature He bears—divine in character. The angels bear a nature quite their own. They are not God nor are they human; they are a creation of God—spiritual beings in a class and for a purpose of ministry all their own. Man never becomes an angel—nor are our dead ever angels.

Then the human nature is below the angelic and is characterized by certain marks which keep it so. And below that is the animal nature and that in turn is bound by certain laws and limitations which hold it as such. Each nature in turn has a structural law and is held by such. The animal never becomes human, neither does the human become angelic. Each retains its identity and potential values.

In making man, or creating him, God said, *"Let us make man in our image, after our likeness."* This refers to a moral and spiritual likeness as suggested by Eph. 4:24; Col. 3:10 and 1 Cor. 11:7. This image is in the form of personality; the stamp God placed upon him lifts man above all lower creation. The lower order is wonderful and many times shows marked signs of intelligence, yet no animal can respond to the appeal and conviction of the Holy Spirit; but fallen man *can* and *does*. The coin was lost, but it still retained the superscription and character of a coin—it did not turn into a potato or a stone. It was out of circulation and failed to fulfill its desired purpose when lost. It may have been a very shiny coin—but lost!

Man in the realm of the human—the fashion in which he was *originally* created, had two characteristic marks which I wish we might remember in relation to his first appearance, as God made him. He was *limited* and *dependent*. Please keep this in mind—he is purposely made so. In the act of creation he is limited, by the structural law of his nature, to do or not to do certain things. He can move and is expected to move only in certain relations because of his design and make-up. He is dependent upon God for life and guidance. He has no life source in himself but has the norm of his being in God. Their wills are still one and he draws life, inspiration and power from the Head—God. He can of himself originate nothing. He may do a thousand and one things, permitted in his power of manifestation, but he is dependent upon God for life and purpose. Let us remember that this limitation was not due to sin, for so far no sin had come to man, the creation of God.

So Adam stands before God, a human being—a man. But listen! do not rest there. He is made for God's glory; that is, God is to be glorified through him; and the image of God, His likeness and character, are to be reflected through him. How? God's plan is revealed. In his make-up as a personality he has, along with his intellectual and emotional life, a strange power vested in him—he has a *will*. In the development of this man *all* departments of his personality are to find expression—he is to grow.

As man stood before God, as we say, a created man— he was just that. But he had neither grown into, nor manifested the hidden, potential values of the human which were in him, which should have come forth in a display of the likeness of God—to the glory of God.

May I help you to see something here. There is a difference between nature and moral character. Adam had the one, human nature, by the act of creation, but not a developed moral character. He was holy and sinless. The human was unfallen, for nature is the result of a free, specific gift, while moral character is the result of testing, proving, discipline and culture. Again we come face to face with a divine law or principle which is always in evidence in the economy and purpose of God, namely—*moral character is built by God only by a process of testing*. It is ever so. Do not quarrel in spirit over this matter. Face it and see it from God's point of view and rejoice. It is one of the divine arrangements. Since it is so, the moral character God desired to see displayed in the unfolding of the human nature in Adam, must be subjected to proof or test. So He places him under probationary law. Gen. 2:16, 17.

Many dear souls think it *unkind* of the Lord to make such a beautiful place, put man in it and then put that forbidden tree in the way. Well, dear child, listen! It was the best and only thing He could do if there ever was to be a display of the purpose in making man. He has a will. How can it be tested if not in a place where it may have *power* to choose right from wrong.? How can you make a choice if there is nothing on which to exercise the power to choose? Therefore we find the test established. To cause Adam to fail? No, to cause him to grow. Friends have asked me, "What do you think would have happened if Adam had not failed in that test?" I believe there would have been another test and still another to *release* the strength and beauty of the moral character, or likeness of God, in a wonderful unfolding by way of the human nature. In the strength of the one test he would have been placed in the next, a continual development and displaying of the image of God. From the very beginning it was God's desire that man should *grow*.

But we must leave Adam, the human, in a total wreck. The failure had a fearful reaction on the whole realm of his make-up. Through that surrender of his will he became a fallen wreck—spirit, soul and body. There was a seeming— only seeming—defeat of God's purpose to see a *man* after His own image. But we shall trace the purpose of God to the satisfaction of His heart. He is *never* defeated.

So let us grow—*"grow in wisdom and knowledge of our Lord and Savior, Jesus Christ."*

10.

THE LAST ADAM

MAN was to exercise his power of choice and in so doing reflect the likeness and image of God. He possessed an unfallen human nature as a gift of God in the act of creation. The moral character or likeness and image of God was to come or be made manifest through a process of testings or trials. This was and still is a principle upon which God works in developing Christian character or likeness to Christ. We found the will of man was one of the three factors included in the study of his personality and was really the one factor at which God continually looks.

Man was to exercise his power of choice and in so doing show its strength in willing *with* God and thus glorifying His Name. In choosing against sin and self and the self-will there is a growth into the likeness of God and a stamping of His nature and image more clearly upon the heart and life where the right choice is made. Thus is ever the process of character building.

Nature, even the new nature at conversion, is a free gift, but the character and likeness of Christ comes as a process of building and growth. This depends upon our power to choose, and so are we continually coming more and more into the likeness of Christ; *"Till we all come in the unity of the faith and of the knowledge of the Son of God, unto a perfect man, unto the measure of the stature of the fulness of Christ."*

So in God's purpose for man He was to have found

99

through this perfect human being a peculiar and special manifestation of His likeness and image as the hidden, potential values of the man unfolded and his will was' exercised under the probationary law of Gen. 2:17.

In the very first test man failed in his whole nature, and he, as both a being and a personality crashed to a level of broken humanity, and was consequently placed under the law of sin and death. God did not find in the first Adam the great desire of His heart. Even the deeper powers of the human creation were never released to His glory. So man, ever since the fall and first failure, has had a poor, broken down creation and nature with which to work. The wonder and miracle to me is to see what he is able to produce even so—but alas! the finest manifestations and products of the same are but colossal ruins of a fallen Adamic creation. That is why, when God saves us, He makes us a *new* creation and expects nothing from the old. We are *new* creatures in Christ—not wash-overs.

In thinking of this matter of God's first purpose and Adam's failure, I like to remember Isaiah 55:11, *"So shall my word be that goeth forth out of my mouth: it shall not return unto me void, but it shall accomplish that which I please, and it shall prosper in the thing whereto I sent it."* Had not God spoken a word? Yes, in Gen. 1:26, *"And God said, Let us make man in our image, after our likeness."* Surely God is not to be defeated. Though the first Adam was a failure, God was yet to see His mighty purpose fulfilled.

This brings us more directly to the study at hand—the Last Adam. Let us remember that names in the Scriptures were always given because they represent or portray character. That is, the name suggests the very character or nature of the one who held it. Among the names given to our blessed Lord, there are two I want to look at in this connection. In 1 Cor. 15:45 He is called, *The Last Adam,* and in 1 Tim. 2:5, He is called *The Man Christ Jesus.* Therefore, He must be unto God a perfect Adam—that is, He is to display and carry to its triumph the original idea for the first Adam. He must be the *ideal* man, a perfect reflection of God's image and likeness, shining and gleaming through the human instrument—the perfect, sinless, faultless, limited and dependent human—even the Last Adam.

Right here let us remember the Law of the Offerings and their order of offering, and we come again to the teaching found in this sermon. You remember the first offering was the Whole Burnt Offering, and was *"a sweet savour unto God"*—*"a male without blemish."* God came *first* and had a peculiar and spiritual satisfaction in this *first* offering—it was *Godward.* Remember Christ's motto: *"Lo! I come to do Thy will."* So in His human aspect and manifestation there is ever that which looks *toward* God, and in return God finds in that life (from the human side) a delight and satisfaction.

Since this discourse has to do with Christ as the Last Adam and Man Christ Jesus, let us look at the question of His incarnation. We must needs do this if we want to understand a little better this marvelous and wonderful Christ. Sometimes in one's desire to defend one phase of truth he becomes over-anxious and refuses to look at other phases or angles of the matter for fear he may not keep true or loyal to the side he sees, and from which he has gained spiritual illumination and inspiration. But this should not be so. The truth has many sides and is universal. No one or no one group has a corner on *all* truth. We are finite, and the glimpses we get are but fragmentary. The whole truth is the Word of God, but we are limited, and only by the Spirit of revelation do we get even the flashes which ever change and revolutionize our lives. We have so long preached and taught His deity and divinity that we have almost forgotten that He *has* a human side and became a partaker of our flesh. If God can say He is the Last Adam and a Man, I must believe it, and see Him as such. Then the Spirit adds much to any conception of Him, and He *draws* me, and ere I know it, I am low at His feet.

Turn with me to Phil. 2:6-8. We cannot expect to do much with this text in this discourse, since it is too heavy and there are too many lines of departure to be considered. Therefore I will confine our study to the use of certain words and so help clear up some mental webs, and maybe we can see a bit more clearly. *"Who being in the form of God,"*—here the word *form* is *morpha,* and means the essential form of being, that which is the very essence of the thing. Here His *morpha* is really His deity—He is God in essence and essential form of being. In verse 6 we read, *"and took upon Him the form (morpha) of a servant."* Note, the Word does not say He was like a servant, or acted like a servant, but *took* the *form* of one. He was in all reality a servant, as Old Testament study will prove. Next, the word *likeness* (verse 7) means the *habit* of mankind. It is a most suggestive word. *"And found in fashion as a man"*—here *fashion* is *schema* and means, *the fashion of life.* So we find Him in truth to be God (in *morpha*); He is the second member of the Trinity. Yet He is a servant and adapts Himself to the habit of man and moves in the fashion of the same.

Now someone wants to know what it was He let go in becoming incarnate in the human form. Some fear at once that if we speak of Him in the human, we deny His deity or place in the Godhead, and so they wonder what He left in order to become man. Yes, He was, is, and ever will be *equal* with God. There was nothing concerning His equality that He left. There are two items to be considered here—neither are divine attributes, and yet both were becoming to Him in His place in the Godhead, namely, (1) peculiar experience at home in that relationship, (2) the glory which was an accompanying feature of the same. These were both relinquished for the time. He lays them aside and becomes the Last Adam, the Man Christ Jesus; *Christ* suggests the divine side—the Anointed of God, while *Jesus* suggests the human aspect and the nature of man.

Perhaps a little illustration here will help: Let us suppose there is up yonder on the mountainside a fine fir tree. All the essential qualities and attributes which hold it under the structural law of the fir tree, make it a fir tree and *nothing* else. All the peculiar, qualifying marks are there, and we know it as a perfect fir tree. That is its *morpha*— its essential being. But suppose we cut it down and place it in our living room as a Christmas tree. In so doing have we changed in any way or form its essential being? Not at all. It is still a fine fir tree. But it now has the *form* of a Christmas tree. It does not *act* like a Christmas tree. It *is* a Christmas tree—the form or morpha of a servant. Do you see? And now go on a little: While it was up on the mountainside it may have stood alone; it may have been in a clump or group with others; it may have been in a rocky place, or maybe near the water, or on some barren height. That was its *schema,* the fashion or arrangement of its setting, its habitat. But now it has a new habitat or fashion, called in verse 7 *likeness,* (habit), and verse 8, *schema.* It is in a room surrounded by furniture and here is the glowing fire, and we hear the music and joyous laughter of the Christmas season. Listen! Is the tree any *less* a fir tree? To have made it bear our gifts and hold the lights, etc., makes it no less the same fir tree, only it is *serving.*

Again, look at a personal illustration: Here I am before you, quite active. Well, that is the way God made me.

I use my body, or rather the Lord does, and in so doing I become an instrument for His service. But suppose you tie me up, hand and foot, and let me minister thus. Tied up, am I any the less Follette? Absolutely not, only I would find myself extremely limited. And that is exactly what happened when Christ, God's Son—God the I AM, came to us. He was the perfect, limited Man. He crowded and cramped Himself down and lived in our form (*morpha*) and fashion (*schema*). Remember it was the perfect, *unfallen* nature He took. God could not start Him in a broken-down, ruined nature—sinful and marred. Remember Gal. 4:4, 5, *"made of a woman, under the law"*; also Heb. 2:14, 15, *"Forasmuch then as the children are partakers of flesh and blood, he also himself likewise took part of the same; that through death he might destroy him that had the power of death, that is the devil; and deliver them who through fear of death were all their lifetime subject to bondage."* It is beyond us to probe down into this subject. It is too wonderful!

From birth, from the human side, God saw the perfect development and unfolding of the human as it should have been, without sin and failure. All the powers of the human creation—hidden in Adam—find perfect display in Christ Jesus. Three times God breaks through the heavens and gives testimony as to His pleasure (before Jesus ever reaches Calvary). All three times He is in some way touching the matter of His death. Matt. 17:5; Jno. 12:28; Matt. 3:17. Why? He was ever (before the foundation of the world) the *Lamb*. This lamb was to be without spot or blemish—*perfect*. Therefore Christ was to carry the Adamic ideal and scheme to its perfection, and so have a perfect man offered through the obedience and perfection of the Son, the Lamb. Christ must be a perfect man ere He can die. The study of His perfect triumph and victory is most startling, fascinating and amazing. Watch Him from the temple experience, on through. I cannot now trace the steps but they are all there and ravishing to look upon. He perfectly does *what* man failed to do—*to glorify God and do His will.* In John 17 note His approach to God in that marvelous prayer. He does not begin by telling God of His work on Calvary and the redemption of the world. No! Verse 4, *"I have glorified Thee on the earth."* Isn't that grand! God first. God's glory, God's will, God's place first—then—*"I have finished the work which Thou gavest me to do."*

On the Mount of Transfiguration we find Him bringing to its climax the walk of the Last Adam. It took Him thirty-three years to climb that mountain. It took thirty-three years to bring to perfection the ideal man, and as far as Christ's being man was concerned, that was His place of absolute triumph. Man was not originally meant to die—but to have entered into some phase of glorification as here suggested. God breaks through and says, *"I am well pleased."* When no one else could be pleased or could understand, God *was*, and pronounced this great testimony upon an obedient Man, the Son of God.

But He cannot tarry on that mountain. He is now the perfect Lamb without spot or blemish. The Lamb must be offered and so there is another mountain to climb. So He must go down. At the foot of the mountain He finds the demoniac (a type of broken humanity). He picks him up, as it were, and carried him in His bosom, to Calvary. That crazy, undone bit was Follette, and you, and you, and you—we were all there in deep, deep need, crazed and all disorganized by sin. But the mighty, triumphant, all-glorious Christ picked us up and we died in Him!

So the Lamb is slain and Redemption is made a glorious reality. Is He yours? Are you, too, conscious that you

have passed from sin unto life? Now a partaker of Life
with Him? Do not think, from the statement above, that
it took thirty-three years for Christ to perfect the ideal
nature. I am not talking about His human *nature*—that
was always perfect. But during the thirty-three years there
was the perfect and complete *unfolding* of the human so
that in *that* He perfectly glorified the Father. He was the
complete, ideal expression of the Last Adam, the Man
Christ Jesus.

Let us surrender more fully to Him and allow Him to
come more perfectly into a union with us, of faith and
power to also glorify His Name. Surely He is not less
God—He is the mighty God, coming to us in our need
through the Son, the Last Adam, the Man Christ Jesus.

II

PETER BEFORE

THIS afternoon I want to talk to you about Jesus. I want you to see Him in action that you might see how He handles certain situations. He is unique in the way He deals with people because He has such wisdom and tact.

The story I want to take up is found in John 21:1-18. Let us read it over again to refresh our minds and to get a clear picture of the scene. It is a refreshing story because it does not involve any special doctrinal issue, neither is it complicated with too many characters. This is just an ordinary incident and yet is one of the most fascinating pictures of Jesus in His dealings with the human heart. How one can look at Him here and trace His thought and actions in behalf of a needy heart and not love and adore Him is quite beyond me! In this study I want Him to be unveiled, as it were, and to stand before you.

Before we can appreciate this story we must go back a bit and get a clear idea of the background, which is suggested by the first phrase in the story, *"After these things Jesus showed Himself,"* etc. To view the drama, hearing the conversations and watching the actions will not mean very much to us unless we know what has happened to call forth the story. Suppose you should receive a letter starting off, "After all these things had happened," etc., and then following with some interesting doings of your friends, you would doubtless say, "How strange! I do not know what my friends have been doing so how can I get any

connection to make this letter mean something to me?" It
is the same with this story. If we fail to know some of
these things, it reduces itself to merely a passing incident.
As a rule that is about all that many get out of it. They
find here a miracle (which, after all, is about the last thing
to be considered) and they also find Peter being reinstated
after his failure. Both are here but if that is all, *why* introduce the story by, *after these things?* Well, many things
had happened as you know. I want to call your attention
to one thing which influenced the disciples to take the attitude they did. Then let us refer to two incidents in the
life of Peter which, if known in connection here, make the
story alive and radiant. Here is a brilliancy of heart life
and light captivating in its subtle suggestion. Here we must
not only hear words but keep our eyes open to see the
seemingly artless action of the characters.

First of all, what is the heart mood of these disciples
as they take this fishing trip? Of course, they are disciples
of the Lord and we would naturally expect them to be
strong in faith since they have been with Him for three
years, heard His messages and seen His miracles—and then,
too, there is nothing like a personal contact and fellowship to make us understand. They were privileged people.
And certainly, after He has accomplished His death and
resurrection, their hearts ought to be buoyed up and
bounding with faith and great hope. But what is the
real situation? These disciples had suffered a terrific
blow; their hearts were sorely disappointed; their vision
had faded and the hope which they had entertained had
been dashed to the ground and they knew no way out
of their difficulty. Not having understood His message,
from its truly spiritual side, they were at a loss to adjust themselves to the present seeming failure.

Let us remember that Jesus had been continually preaching to them about the Kingdom. This Kingdom idea (of course always to *them* a physical matter) was most welcome. They were weary and tired of foreign tyranny and longed for Israel's national life to be restored and the privilege of showing to the other nations her power and glory. They were *Kingdom conscious,* as it were, and interpreted His visitation, message, and miracles in the light of a manifest Kingdom soon to be set up. This is evidenced by such incidents as the ambitious mother seeking a place for her sons; the desire among themselves to be great in the kingdom; the wish to make Him a King by force; and other occasions when they asked Him if He would not then restore the Kingdom.

Since this was the mental attitude and general conception, much of Jesus' teaching about the character of the subjects of the Kingdom, and motives, and *the Kingdom being within you* did not please them. They had to listen to His words about suffering and death but they did not like it and even rebuked Him for speaking thus. They lived daily in the hope that He would inaugurate the Kingdom and place them in positions of authority and power.

Finally He dies. What a shock! But He is resurrected from the dead and appears to them. Hope faintly stirs and once more they look to Him to fulfill His promise. But His visitations were not so very satisfactory, for He disappears almost as soon as He comes. Thus He leaves them again wondering. This is the third time He shows Himself. So let us not be too harsh in our judgment of them. Shall we not learn the lesson of tolerance? Let us put ourselves where they were and erase all we know of the glorious history of Christ and think if perhaps we would not have done as they did. In heart they wanted to love and trust the Lord but they could not figure out this seeming failure. Did you never have your mind in confusion over something you had all the time hoped was of the Lord? We must be patient with them. Now comes a perfectly natural and logical reaction. They are human and the whole procedure is what one would naturally expect. They have not the faith to wait or to pray it through so they do the next thing—they try to think it through. There are many things in life we shall never be able to think through, but we may pray them through.

This is always true in the matter of spiritual truth and revelation. Mysteries are not discerned with the mind but with the heart. Faith reaches out by the Spirit of revelation and thereby touches the invisible until it becomes more real to us than the ground we tread upon. Through the spirit of revelation we can touch the mysteries of God until they feed and refresh our hearts. These poor men were sick, sore, and disappointed in heart. The thing had not worked out as they had hoped it would. Have you ever been disappointed? Have you, too, been shocked to find what all the time you thought was *His* way, was some personal idea and desire of your own heart? How many times we put our own interpretation on some word He has given, to please ourselves in the realm of our own desires! Then when it does not come to pass, if we are not careful, everyone else is to blame. The disciples were all the time interpreting the spiritual and heavenly things in terms of bread and butter, in terms of a material kingdom. Of course, they will not go to the pit for this; but had they learned their lesson sooner they might have been spared much heartache.

Now what else had happened? We find in this story that Jesus deals with one person, Peter. He is the star actor in the little drama. Let us make a brief study of Peter. Why do we find introduced in the story such factors as fish nets, a fire and coals, and the conversation *just* as it is? What has *after these things* to do with Peter?

Let us look at Luke 22:24-34. There had been a strife
as to power and position, a bit of politics, only of course
the Bible does not call it that. But nevertheless there had
been a discussion about position and relationship in the
Kingdom. Jesus discerned it. They were not lovingly saying, "I prefer you to have the highest honor. Since I
have been with our Lord and Master His spirit of love
and sacrifice have become a part of me. When He sets
up His Kingdom I want to show you how much I am
like Him so I want *you* to have all the honor He can
give you. Even that which He may offer me." Then Jesus
teaches them a lesson as to what *greatness* is in His sight.
Quite a rebuke to the popular and material idea, I am
sure.

Then He speaks to Peter. The force of verse 31 is
better understood from a translation by Weymouth. It is
nearer the thought as given in the original Greek. *"Simon,
Simon, I tell you that Satan has obtained permission to
have all of you to sift as wheat is sifted; but I have prayed
for you that your faith may not fail, and you, when at
last you have come back to your true self, must strengthen
your brethren."* So you see from this reading that *all*
were to have their siftings. But we are privileged to get
a glimpse of Peter only in his. And we, too, are to have
our siftings. Surely we are no better than they. I am
very conscious of the need of it, are you not? Here we
find Jesus so tender in His dealings. But note the effect
upon Peter. Now standing in the sufficiency of his own
flesh and what he thinks is devotion and love, he dares
to declare it: *"Master, with you I am ready to go both
to prison and to death."* This is what I call a boastful and
extravagant confession. Here he makes death the measure
of his love.

How many today have made extravagant prayers? How
marvelous they sound! How easy to say some things when

the Spirit is upon us! What about all this extravagant praying, great desires and high ambitions for God? After all, these fantastic prayers all have to, in the last analysis, pass through the censorship of God's will. God has often dealt with me in my prayer life until it has been recast, remodeled and toned down many times. Don't be afraid to let the Lord deal with you in this matter. He may reduce them as He has mine. He likes short prayers and long faith rather than long prayers and short faith.

This idea of big prayers brings to my mind a student we once had in school. He was a fine fellow and of a strong nature and will. He had received a definite experience (but not the Baptism) and was quite a fine worker even before he came to school. In teaching we were emphasizing such truths as death to self, self-effacement, the place of the Spirit over against nature, humility, etc. But he was full of natural zeal and did not like it. I loved the lad and knew there were rich possibilities there if ever the Lord could get at him. I prayed much for him (and I am afraid he would not have liked *what* I prayed had he known). What a time we had! I knew the lessons ground him all the time but the Lord would not let me change my message to suit his flesh or ideas. I kept right on. One morning when we were praying for the missionaries he became very interested and very much in earnest. Soon he was praying in a loud tone of voice, and by way of emphasis, pounding on a chair bottom, "O God, make us martyrs. Give us the spirit of a martyr. Give us the grace of a martyr."

It all sounded very wonderful; but I knew the dear lad. I knew he perfectly hated to do the dishes when it came his turn on duty. Every time it was his turn to help in the kitchen one would almost think the world was coming to an end. He simply could not get the victory over a dishpan. When I heard him praying so intensely that morning I felt like poking him and saying, "Never mind, dear, you do not need to pray to be a martyr, for God never makes one out of your kind of material. If you can not get victory over a dishpan you will never need victory to be a martyr." But I kept still. I wonder sometimes if the matter of getting victory over a dishpan is not as great in God's sight as some more spectacular thing which wins the applause of men.

Finally this boy went out into the work and learned some hard lessons. The Lord was not through with him, for he was a choice vessel, and as you know, choice instruments have to suffer much sometimes. All the time I was teaching I could feel a resentment in his spirit although we never had a word. He was kind and polite and obedient but I knew he did not like the truth. He thought he didn't like *me* and felt (what he thought was) my personality grinding on him. I knew it was not my personality but the truth. He did not see a very important thing for all of us to see in this matter, namely, the difference between personality and truth. I will show you what I mean in a moment.

Never confuse the truth with the instrument. Sometimes people do and are converted to a person and not to Christ or Truth. So when the person fails, the poor dear soul is swept off his feet. After several years in the school of the Spirit, this boy met me. The very first thing he did was to grab me and give me a most terrific bear hug. And as he did so he was crying and saying,

"Oh, Follette, I love you now! I love you and know what you were saying. Oh, Follette, isn't it all wonderful?"

Today he is a strong, fine worker and God's seal is upon him in marked fashion. I am sure, too, that he is not praying about martyrdom—but something very much nearer where he is living. Thank God! So let us not pray extravagant prayers. Don't bother asking God for grace for such things when you can't get victory over a dishpan or something less. To get a victory over as small a thing as that, is often a test of real character and faith. So Peter had been making some very bold and extreme statements about his love and devotion to his Lord.

12

PETER AFTER

THE second incident which I think is *one* of *these things* spoken of in the opening phrase, is found in John 18:15-19. Here is the sad picture of Peter's failure. He has denied his Lord and is now among His enemies. He has made a fearful botch of the whole thing. What a failure after a close and happy walk with Jesus for three years! What a revelation!

How could it all be true? But Jesus is not through with Peter; He wants to get hold of him and help him. So, in the permissive will of God, he is thrown over very close to the enemy, so close that the enemy can grab hold of him and even shake him good. He is put into a sieve, and Jesus knew all about it. Note the tenderness of Jesus as He deals with this known weakness of Peter's. He helps him as far as He is able. He says, as it were,

"Peter, you are about to suffer a terrific humiliation and testing. I cannot pray for your exemption; the Father does not give me the liberty to pray for that. I cannot pray that you be spared the pain and agony of it. Your very nature and disposition demand this very treatment and experience. However, Peter, I may pray one thing and that I will do with all my faith and power. I will pray that your faith *fail not*. I will pray that it may not snap under the horrible fire of testing but that it may come out strengthened and made vigorous for the days to come."

115

Have you ever had Jesus pray you through? Jesus prayed for Peter in that terrific trial he was to suffer. Jesus did not blame him for it. He knew his makeup and that it was the only way for Peter, so He loved him and prayed him through. By nature we are all a part of the colossal ruin of man. We are all cast in a broken mold and God knows it. But we can become new creatures in Christ, thank God! He wants to come in and move through the different departments of our personalities and show to the world a miracle of His grace in the display of His power in and through us.

Returning again to Peter, we find that after he has made his two rash and extravagant statements, he falls down on both of them. But the Lord had allowed it all. "Oh," you say, "the Lord would never order his steps thus." Yes, He certainly would when He sees it is for Peter's good. Do you think the Lord wanted Peter as he was before that trial? Certainly not. (Did not Paul need a demon to torment him? Many think it would have been wonderful if Paul could have gotten a victory over the demon. He won many other victories but he never was free from the stake. No, he needed the stake as a safety device to keep him in position. He did more than have a prayer answered; he got grace to carry him all the days he had to tarry.)

Up to this time God could not do much with Peter even though he had followed Jesus and knew His message and was called. God wanted more than that. He wanted Peter and could not get him, only through this trial. So Jesus prays him through and poor Peter feels so humiliated and ashamed.

Now we shall better understand Peter's mood when the story takes place. When the disappointment of Christ's disappearance and failure to bring in the Kingdom settled down upon the disciples, what did they do? A perfectly natural thing. When your faith cannot bridge the chasm, when it is not strong enough to take the step, you will always resort to some natural means of escape. That is the way we are made. When faith fails then we begin struggling and working and leaning upon the resources of nature. The disciples did this very thing. Peter is the spokesman. I know we sometimes ridicule him for talking so much but I am sure we are glad many times that he said what he did. Many times he saves us the trouble of asking or saying the very thing we are happy he has said. Every once in a while I learn a lesson from what Peter has done. So I have to say, "Thank you, Peter!" No doubt most of them thought as he did in their hearts. At least none of them had a suggestion as to a way out.

I can imagine Peter looking at the rest and saying, "Well, this kingdom business has not turned out as I had expected. I have been thinking: Don't you remember the day He said, *'The kingdom of God cometh not with observation'?* And again, *'The kingdom is within you'?* Then see how He has died and gone. Now He has shown Himself twice but how do we know if He will ever come back again? This kingdom, it seems to me, is too mystical. And, as you know, I never was mystically inclined. I guess I don't understand it. But I do know something about fishing. So, as for me, I am going fishing. You may do as you like. This whole kingdom idea is exploded and has ended in a crash. I may have gotten into some kind of emotionalism, but I tell you, I am going back to my nets."

That is why Peter went fishing. It was not because he thought the fish would bite. It was something worse than that. I really do not think he cared much whether or not there was a fish in the sea. He just wanted to get away, away, away from the whole thought and atmosphere of the past years and days. He did not want to be haunted by too many thoughts and suggestions from his

friends. He wanted a change of environment! Do any of
you know what I mean?

Instantly the others say, "We, too, will go. You have
always been a leader and there seems to be nothing else to
do so we will go along." They, too, probably wanted a
change but did not own up to it. I wonder what the dear
Lord read in their hearts just then? So there they are,
out there fishing! fishing! fishing! The night settles down
and they fish on and on. It comes to be one o'clock and
there are no fish; two o'clock and no fish. They try
every old haunt they have ever known; this point, that
bank, this little cove and that, all the old holes they have
been in before. It is cold and the nets are heavy and
hard to handle. Oh, the emptiness of it all! Poor dears,
they are on grounds from which He has called them. Did
you ever walk over the old paths? Have you felt the
haunting spirit of such a place? How many banks and
shoals will you try before you give up? We read that
they fished all night and caught nothing. But listen—
*"But when the morning was now come, Jesus stood on the
shore."* Thank God, there is always a morning! There
they are, a wretched, forlorn, unhappy, disheartened little
group. They had no business in the boat at all for He
had called them from their nets to make them fishers
of men.

The night cannot last too long. Finally there is a faint
streak of light over against the hills and it continues to
grow a bit lighter. The mist and fog are hanging along
the shore so that only a dim outline of things is visible.
But as they look they see someone moving about and
finally they hear a voice calling, *"Children, have you any
meat?"* In other words, "Have you caught anything?" Jesus
takes the initiative and that by asking a question. Why
that particular one? Why not scold them and rebuke them?
Are they not out of order? Do they not need to be lined

up? Yes, yes, yes, but please wait and let the Lord do it.
He knows how. How many of you think that Jesus did
not know about the boat or if they had any fish or not?
If for a moment you think He asked merely for informa-
tion, you are much mistaken. He had in mind the blessing
of a deliverance and the reinstating of Peter and his commission. But He must first ask them this question. He
must build the blessing upon a certain foundation and that
foundation is a confession. Have you not yet learned in
the Christian experience that *confession is the basis of
blessing?*

He knew all their circumstances but He wanted this
one thing: a confession of their defeat and failure in their
self-will. He wanted them to own up to the failure and
that in most simple form—*"Nothing."* How much better to
make a clean breast of it than to say, "If the wind had
not flapped the sails or if so-and-so had not rocked the
boat, I think we might have caught some." Thank God,
they said in simple form, "Nothing." As soon as He gets
this confession He builds up a blessing and directs them
as to what to do. Now in obedience they are fishing in
the very same boat, the very same water, with the very
same nets and in the very same place. But what a change!
The fish just could not get into the nets cast in *disobedience,* neither can they keep out of the nets cast in
obedience. It is not a matter of water or place—just His
word. Then He bids them come to shore.

Here He has a happy surprise for them. How very wise
and tactful Jesus is! See how delicately and carefully He
handles Peter! Even though Jesus is tender and tactful,
He does not intend to let Peter get by, as we say. He
never does. His very love is manifested in correction. He
loves Peter dearly and is going to deal with him in a
most clever and sweet way without causing him embarrassment before his fellow disciples. But at the same time

He will so deal with Peter that he will never forget it.
So the Lord has some coals of fire and fish for them.
And as the disciples come up I can imagine the Lord
saying, "Peter, won't you come and warm yourself? Here
is a fine fire and you must be cold and damp."

The very mention of a fire must have set Peter thinking
and remembering. The fire of his conscience was hotter
than any fire there. Where had he warmed himself just
a while before this? Had it not been at the fire of Jesus'
enemies? And had he not grouped himself with them? Were
not Jesus and Peter thinking of that fire, too? I think so.
Do you not think Peter got warm? Surely he must have
been warmed through and through. The Lord had not
rebuked him by a word, neither had He done one thing
to embarrass him before the others. But He had sent
home to Peter such a rebuke that I am sure he never
forgot it. It was His kindness that hurt Peter. Then I
seem to hear the Lord say, "Shall we now have a little
breakfast? Were there not some fish that you caught?"
Do you remember who went for them? To be sure it was
Peter. My! how he must have fairly run to get them.
And to get away from that *very hot fire*. He needed a
cool breath of air by that time.

So he leaves the fire but it has accomplished its purpose in warming more than Peter's hands. Oh, how hard
Peter was thinking as He saw the Lord moving about
and directing, such seemingly simple words, and yet at
the same time getting at him in such untold fashion. And
now, how could poor Peter eat? Was there not a lump
in his throat nigh choking him? Yet the Lord hands
him some fish and asks him to eat with Him. I am sure
Peter never disliked fish in all his life as he did just then.
How it must have choked him! Busy in his mind with
thoughts the other disciples never dreamed of—"Oh, Lord,
I am such a failure! I have grieved Your heart and

disappointed You. I am so miserable and undone. My
heart is broken and I am so ashamed. Yet, oh Lord, I
need You and I so want to run to You and tell You! Oh,
Lord, how can You be kind to me? How can You spread
a feast for me? Rather would I that You blame me,
scold me. I deserve it! Oh, Jesus, will You ever let me
get close to You again? Can You ever trust me with
Your love and fellowship?" Poor Peter! The others were
having a fine, warm breakfast. Well, let them eat. That
is about all some ever get.

Jesus has no rebuke for Peter. Instead He enters into
a conversation as casually as in days of old. He does
not show by any gesture that there is anything the matter.
His looks and spirit do all that is necessary. After they
have eaten He says, *"Peter, lovest thou me more than these?"*
Some think He was referring to the fish since he had
denied the Lord and left his great calling to catch them.
But we find in the Greek that the word *these* does not
refer to the fish but to the others standing by. But why
should He ask that? Had Peter not told Him twice that
he loved Him more than *that* even to the measure of
death? Yes, so Jesus keeps it fresh in His mind. Does it
seem foolish and meaningless that the Lord should have
said over and over three times, *"Lovest thou me,"* etc?
But Jesus did not say that. Read it in the original. There
you will find two different words for *love* are used. One
is *agapao* and means a love, deep and of a sacrificial
measure. It is the strongest word in Greek for *love,* the
one used to show God's love for the world, etc. The other
word is *fileo.* This means to be very dear, and to be fond
of, and is used to show affection such as brotherly love
and feeling. It is a weaker word than the other.

Jesus is just wise enough to use the very word that
would characterize the statement Peter had made. So He
says, *"Peter, (agapao) lovest thou me?"* etc. He uses the

strong word, for had not Peter declared his love in such lofty terms? Doubtless Peter's failure had taught him a lesson. He had found by now that he did not love Him to the extent that he would die for Him. Peter knows what the Lord is getting at and in answer says, "Lord, Thou knowest that I (*fileo*) am very fond of Thee." He does not dare again to use the extravagant word he once used. Jesus takes the confession for what it is worth and says, "*Feed my lambs.*" Again, the second time Jesus speaks and says, "*Peter,* (*agapao*) *lovest thou Me?*" He again uses the strong word. Peter does some deep thinking. He answers the Lord, "Thou knowest, Lord, I am very fond of Thee," using the weaker word again. And all this time the disciples do not seem to know just what it is all about. A third time Jesus speaks, "Simon, son of Jonas"—and here we get a beautiful lesson. When we cannot measure up to the strong place He would have us reach, He comes down to us and meets us in the measure of love of which we are capable. So this time Jesus says, "Are you very fond of me?" or "Am I dear to you?" This breaks poor Peter and he confesses, "Yes, Lord, Thou knowest I am fond of Thee. Thou knowest everything." Three times he failed the Lord and denied Him, and three times he confesses afresh his love for Him.

It was all the Lord wanted. He gained the victory in Peter and yet never rebuked him before the others or made him ashamed before them.

Look, too, at a very clever or wise thing He does for Peter. I am sure those disciples were very human. Do you not think they had spoken of Peter's failure one to another? Behind his back no doubt they said, "My! poor Peter! Wasn't that a dreadful failure? What a dreadful thing! We must pray for him; he needs prayer." Yes, he did, but it was not theirs that got the victory. The Lord knew their inner feelings and thoughts. Therefore before them all, so that they could hear and have the benefit of it all, He reinstates Peter and gives him a three-fold, divine commission.

I wonder if the disciples might not have done a little thinking just then? They, too, had a gentle rebuke for any secret thought they might have entertained. Oh, of course, they did not say anything. It is never wise to do that. But the Lord saw to it (for some reason) that they heard Him bless Peter and again entrust him with His love and message. Have you ever been criticized, misjudged or lied about? It is wonderful just to *"stand still and see the salvation of God."* He can in a most wonderful way close the mouths of those who do not understand and bless you in their very presence. Is He not wonderful? How safe He is in dealing with a needy heart! Shall we not love Him and trust Him more? Can we not all of us afresh commit to His tender, tactful, and wise dealings the welfare of our foolish hearts?

THE CALL OF DEEP UNTO DEEP

D own in the depth of my nature
Where the issues of life are born,
From that unknown mystical realm,
Surviving through ages of storm,
A call is forever rising—
But its language I cannot speak.
It was born ere I had being,
'Tis the call of deep unto deep.

Our mother tongue here is awkward,
For no words can fully express
The needs in the depths of nature,
In bondage to sin and distress.
Our hearts in their depths sorely ache;
They hunger; they call; and they seek—
Then silently wait an answer
To the call of deep unto deep.

Down deep in the heart of our God,
In mystical regions sublime,
In the Godhead's holy council
Long before our world or our time,
An answer was fully prepared
Every pain, every ache to meet,
In Christ, God's only begotten,
Is answer to deep unto deep.

The Answer indeed was the Word,
The Word when expressed was the Son.
Oh language of God how profound!
In answer what more could be done?
The heart of our God is hungry,
His portion, His people to seek.
"I thirst," was cried by the Answer—
'Tis the call of deep unto deep.

—John Wright Follette

13.

DEEP CALLETH UNTO DEEP

"Deep calleth unto deep at the noise (call) of thy water-spouts: all thy waves and thy billows are gone over me."
Psalm 42:7.

ALTHOUGH this Psalm is not purely Messianic we find in verse seven a most impressive and suggestive prophecy of Christ in His work of redemption. The picture is that of the boundless ocean evidently in great commotion. It is storm-swept. Its waves are lashed into fury and as they heave and rock, the wind sweeps down and whirls the water into gigantic waterspouts thus discovering deep vacuums which yawn and, as it were, call one to another. Into the midst of this awful confusion and wild fury a helpless soul is cast and while the waves and billows sweep over and over him, his voice is raised in agony. Mingled with the boom and roar of the storm we hear him call out, *"Deep calleth unto deep at the noise of thy waterspouts: all thy waves and thy billows are gone over me."*

It is needless to say that this refers to Christ. The primary and supreme interpretation is that it represents Christ swallowed up in the judgments of God. These are the billows of divine wrath from a holy God striking upon and swallowing up its victim. It is the bleeding, helpless Lamb upon the cross where the just wrath of God smote sin and forever rendered the enemy a defeated foe. Who can ever estimate the suffering, agony and terror of that awful hour? We shall never know what

125

it meant to have all of God's waves and billows go over Him that we might have salvation.

Here is another interpretation, mentioned by the Editor of *Elbethel*, which is very suggestive and helpful. She shows how *deep calling unto deep* represents one unknown *depth of need* in our hearts moved upon by God and calling to another. This is so true. As he moves upon one "deep" in nature it calls for movement upon another and thus is God doing a deepening work in the hearts and lives of His children today. The waterspouts are means used by God in this wonderful work. His ways are not pleasing to the natural but are most effectual when permitted to work out His purpose for us.

One day the Lord brought this verse to my attention with still another application and lesson. It was soon after visiting the Grand Canyon in Arizona and I think for that reason it spoke with freshness of meaning. It was there that the significance of *depth* dawned upon my natural sense. I believe this canyon is considered the most sublime of all earthly spectacles. Even a most superficial description of the enormous abyss may hardly be put into words.

Standing upon the rim one overlooks a thousand square miles of pyramids and minarets, carved from painted depths. Many miles away and more than a mile below his feet, the tourist sees a tiny silver thread which he knows to be the giant Colorado. Imagine a stupendous chasm, in places from ten to thirteen miles wide from rim to rim, more than two hundred miles long in all of its meanderings, and more than a mile deep! I shall not presume to tell of its mysterious beauty—strange and unearthly. It is never the same. The colors change with every changing hour; it is ever undergoing transformation. The lights and shades, mists, filmy rainbow veils, cloud fleeces, and purple shadows all move in perfect harmony of mass and color.

It quite outstretches the faculty of measurement. At times it is a brooding, terrible thing, unflinchingly real, yet spectral as a dream. I only mention the Canyon because to my own heart and mind it gave me fresh apprehension of *depth*—but depth only in the natural.

THE FIRST DEEP

Now let us turn to the meaning of our text as it came to my heart after seeing something of such majestic heights and depths. *Deep calleth unto deep!* The first deep mentioned, speaks of the unutterable and fathomless depths of the human heart. It is that mysterious, subtle, under-region or ocean floor of man's heart. In the natural he moves about upon the surface and only occasionally is aware of its hidden possibilities. In Proverbs 4:23 we find it is the source from which are the issues of life. It is not the place of manifestation and actual expression, but where issues are *born* which in time find their way to the surface and come into notice. It is that desperate need incurred by the sin and fall of the whole race in Adam.

What is the character of this strange deep? What could be the *nature* of such an unexplored and foreboding region? Jeremiah 17:9 tells us it is *deceitful above all things, and desperately wicked*. Jeremiah, even though a prophet, was baffled at the thought of sounding it or telling in detail its workings. It was enough in his estimation to say as he did in the original, "it is desperately sick and incurable." Then he adds, *Who can know it?*

Dear friends, we may perhaps measure the Grand Canyon and with the scientific instruments of today sound its depth and magnificent dimensions. We are appalled and silenced before such majestic workings of God. Our feeble sense of distance even here is too weak to comprehend—and this is but a little of His handiwork. Could we measure the *deep* mentioned in the text? No apparatus, however ingeniously constructed, ever finds the hidden springs of the human heart. Thank God, it is not given man to know. He has nowhere told us to try so impossible and dispiriting a task.

To begin with, man has not the correct estimation of distance in regard to the depth mentioned here, neither has the honesty of heart to read truthfully even the few feet which at times he finds open to his gaze. My heart takes courage to know there is One who does know. There is One who is able to descend down, down, down, even to the bottom of the heart and there discern the need in all its details, of sin, pain, agony, misery, and want. Such work is left to Him. I am not called upon to venture down into such a hazardous pit. In 1 Chronicles 28:9 we find that *"The Lord searcheth all hearts and understandeth all the imaginations of the thoughts."* We find the same truth in Psalm 44:20, 21: *"If we have forgotten the name of our God, or stretched out our hands to a strange god; Shall not God search this out? for He knoweth the secrets of the heart."* In Psalm 139:1, 2, we find David's testimony: *"O Lord, thou hast searched me and known me. Thou knowest my downsitting and mine uprising, thou understandest my thoughts afar off."*

Then in the same Psalm David prays, *"Search me, O God, and know my heart; try me and know my thoughts."* Do you think he prayed this before he had discovered the first shadows and the clouds of darkness over the rim of his own heart? I believe he prayed it *after* he had been convinced in his own soul that *he* was not equal to it and no doubt feared the depths hidden there. So in faith and courage (it takes courage) he prayed that God might do the searching.

Maybe some of us have been searching, and feebly and tremblingly trying to descend into this unspeakable and dingy deep, crowded with shadows, mist and haunting sounds. I dare say that all, at times, have ventured over the rim and really meant it as a pious act to convince our hearts that (out of Christ) we are hopelessly undone and altogether miserable. Pungent conviction of the Holy Ghost is most wholesome and conducive to spiritual growth. But I have never yet met a Christian who tried (alone) to descend those depths but that he ended in hopeless, morbid, introspection; and his faith failing him, he became self-centered.

Since God has told us that such work belongs to Him, let us not try to become holier or deeper in God by unnecessary and uncalled for self-humiliation. There are in this *deep* hidden things—sin, pride, duplicity, unbrokenness, unyieldedness, self-complacency, weakness, and fear. Only God knows all the unutterable possibilities. Were it not for the grace of God and the life of Jesus, where would any of us be today? I am a firm believer in the total depravity of the natural man. I believe the *deep* of need found in the human heart (even in each one) holds the possibilities of any sin, no matter how heinous, were one to be placed in an environment needed to foster its growth and the power of the Blood and restraining influence of the Holy Spirit lifted.

This is surely not a pleasant picture. No one delights in rehearsing the failures of the old creation. I mention it only because it is truth, and to rejoice with my fellow-Christians in the revelation of Christ as the mighty Deliverer. Some are afraid we may not know the deformity and desperate need found in this first *deep* mentioned. They ask if this question is not to be dealt with. Yes, friends, this *deep* is to be considered; but with more adequate skill and intelligence of mind than we have. As Christians we now have the mighty Holy Spirit to do this very work for us. Romans 8:27—"*And He that searcheth the*

*hearts knoweth what is the mind of the Spirit, because He
maketh intercession for the saints according to the will of
God."*

I believe that the blessed Holy Spirit, as part of His
ministry, comes as a mighty Intercessor for us in behalf
of the deep need found in us. We are persuaded that we
are unable to cope with it. Only failure and God's grace
can bring us to such a commendable position. Then He
comes in, and moves down, down, down into those hidden
caverns, down into the crevices, and breathless depths, down
upon the oceanfloor of this unknown deep. There He dis-
cerns the need, and clearly and faithfully reads what to
us is only a groan or agony. Then with mighty intercession, with groanings which cannot be uttered, He brings
those needs before God and prays us through.

Glory to God! Do you wonder that the Spirit prays
through us? Since God gave me a revelation (in part, at
least) of my heart, I am not surprised that the Holy Spirit
was poured through me in groaning and intercession. O
friends, let us praise the Holy Spirit for such gracious
ministry. Isn't He precious?—the tender, undefiled, dove
of God, the delicate, pure, sweet breath of God! How can
He come into this deep? How can He move down into
such unspeakable poverty and bring to the surface the
need and pray it through? O friends, I do not know. The
mystery of godliness is beyond us. But I *do* know He
has come. Hallelujah! If we would yield to Him more
He would do more praying and thus do a deeper cleans-
ing.

What is it that issues from this deep? A cry. How long
has the cry gone up? Since the beginning. For ages it
has come from the broken, bleeding, sinning hearts of mankind, lost, undone, helpless, and needing God. Not only has
it come up from the human breast, but *the whole creation
groaneth and travaileth in pain together until now.* Up

from this first *deep* mentioned comes an agonizing cry for God! God! God!! That is the greatest need in the world today. People think they need so many things—better national life, better politics, better social conditions, better schools, better homes, etc. This is only too true, but the deep need of man is *God*. The blindness of mankind is heart breaking. Too many are *playing* at life on the surface when they might be *living* with God where all these needs might be supplied in Him. Life without God is indeed a tragedy.

THE SECOND DEEP

Now a word as to the second *deep* mentioned in the text. As we found the first *deep* that of need in the human heart, so we find the second *deep* the corresponding supply in the great heart of God. It is the deep, mystical and sublime heart of Jehovah. Who knows its depth? The Psalmist tells us in Psalm 92:5, *"O Lord, how great are thy works; and thy thoughts are very deep."*

Time or space do not permit us to trace or even suggest the unmeasurable depths of God's love. Even the first ingredient in the nature of God is quite beyond our understanding. The depths of wisdom veiled from the mind of man, the hidden counsels of His heart, the unsounded oceans of His grace, the deep places of His being, shrouded in mystery are only faintly dreamed of by mortal mind. Do you wonder that Paul wrote as he did? When a revelation of His grace came to him, he was overpowered and gazing, as it were, off upon the dim outlines of God's salvation and purposes for man, as he comes into the new creation, he cries, *"O the depths of the riches both of the wisdom and knowledge of God! how unsearchable are his judgments and his ways past finding out! For who hath known the mind of the Lord? Or who hath been His counsellor?"* (*Rom.* 11:33).

Again in Eph. 3:18 and 19 Paul tells of the nature of this second deep. *"May be able to comprehend with all saints what is the breadth, and length, and depth, and height; and to know the love of Christ, which passeth knowledge, that ye might be filled with all the fulness of God."*

There is an accompanying hunger on the part of God that He might find expression for His love and an object upon which He might lavish it. We sometimes forget that God has an object in quest. In Deut. 32:9 we read, *"For the Lord's portion is His people."* This is a strange statement. Could not the God of the universe find satisfaction or delight with the angelic hosts? with some celestial order of beings? Could not the marvelous display of creative power in matchless order and grandeur fill His heart with satisfaction? No, friends. We are humiliated to learn that the omnipotent God, Creator of the heavens and the earth, finds peculiar delight in the hearts of His people.

O, how wonderful are the ways of God! Can it be that in my little, cramped, uneventful life God should take pleasure? Yes, dear ones, if we are God's people, we are then His portion which He this very day is seeking. The deep of His heart is calling to the deep in ours. Hallelujah! I saw this afresh in reading the words of Christ, the bleeding Lamb, as He hung upon the cross in dying love, *I thirst*. How potent with meaning! So simple a word veiled unspeakable soul-thirst on the part of Jesus. I am sure the physical body was fever-worn, and pain-racked and from those parched lips came the cry, *I thirst*. But let us not read the surface meaning only. He voiced in such a strange and hidden way the real agony of His soul. Indeed He thirsted. But not alone for water, but O, infinitely more, that the full revelation of His life and death might come even to you and to me. It was the great heart of God "in Christ reconciling the world unto Himself."

We cannot help but ask, In the face of this *deep calleth unto deep,* is there no answer? O, friends, can you imagine a call going up from the deep of human need for ages, and then of the call going out continually from the heart of God and think there could be *no* answer? Thank God there is no such mockery in His plan. The marvelous scheme of salvation not only includes this strange call of *deep unto deep,* but it carries also the answer.

The deep of the human heart had not yet learned to call when God shaped that answer. He needed only to speak one word. In order that we as mortals might understand the language of God, when He spoke that word, *"it became flesh and dwelt among us"* (*John* 1:1, *also* 14).

The answer which God gives to the call from the deep in us is one word, *Jesus.* That is enough. Is there a call today from some deep place in your life? Let me tell you again—*Jesus* is the answer. There can be no need of spirit, soul or body but that one answer may be given—*Jesus, Jesus, Jesus.* Can we ever learn this lesson? Think not that God is ever going to speak another answer. *"For He spake, and it was done; He commanded, and it stood fast"* (*Psalm* 33:9). This is the most costly and marvelous word God ever spoke. It is enough. As a thousand cries go up from our deep, we need only God's answer, *Jesus.*

Now just a word as to the waterspouts. Did you notice that the waterspouts are the occasion for the calling? A waterspout is a whirlwind out upon the water, raising great masses of it to considerable heights. How this speaks again of the work of the Holy Spirit. In Scripture He is spoken of under the symbols of wind and water. Here it is a strong figure—wind and water both in intense action. This is the mighty movement of the Holy Spirit upon the ocean of our lives. As the mass of water is whirled up into the air an immense vacuum is created. This seeks to be filled as in nature a vacuum always does. Thus we have a call. The *deep* becomes, as it were, vocal and begins to call to be filled. Has He not swept over your heart-life many a time in a spiritual cyclone and swept out great depths to be filled?

Praise God for the waterspouts! They are only the agents in the hands of an omnipotent God, destined not to destroy but to "make room." And as on the rolling sea the deeps are discovered by this strange phenomenon and the winds rush in to fill the vacuum, so will the Holy Ghost, like a mighty rushing wind, sweep into our troubled hearts and fill the vacancy and yawning deep. At the noise (call) of *Thy* waterspouts. Many times we think it is a cyclone sent by the devil; or we see the agents only. Thus when our vision is too local we miss the filling because we fail to recognize that the call is from one of His waterspouts.

So, dear ones, may we afresh yield to His working and not only let the call go up from our hearts (voiced, I trust, by the Spirit), but may we take courage in knowing the answer is waiting and will come back in comfort, rest, strength or grace as the *deep* in our natures may demand. Let us yield, that the surface and the shallowness may be displaced by God's waterspouts, creating within us such depths as shall receive the deep things of God.

So doing, the sea of life is sure to be storm swept, not always smooth as the natural may desire; but let us remember He is Sovereign of the sea and that the life committed to Him is safe.

14.

SUBSTANCE AND EVIDENCE

"Now faith is the substance of things hoped for, the evidence of things not seen." (Heb. 11:1).

FAITH makes the unseen things for which we hope, certain to the soul. Concerning faith we must always remember three things. These are true in any case when faith is to be exercised. First, the object of faith must be *beyond the seizure of the senses,* and beyond the field of natural or human achievement. Were it not so faith would be quite unnecessary, for sight or nature would accomplish the desired end. Natural impossibility is the atmosphere in which faith works.

Second, the unseen object of faith must be *hoped for.* That is, the object of faith is a personal desire or ideal or objective which calls out the heart. Here we touch the realm of motives. There is always the motive to be considered as a normal feature of faith. The will alone may not lay hold of the invisible ideal or object, the motive or heart yearning must be there also. Gal. 5:6. *"Faith which worketh by love."* Here we find the motive of faith that really accomplishes things for God.

Third, there must be the personal *conviction* which leads to the venture or move on the part of the individual. He is convinced that the object is not a vagary, but an object as real as any object seen.

I want to consider two words which have sometimes caused confusion and made faith a bugbear when it should be the normal breath of a Christian. We say the substance of this book I hold is paper, ink, thread, etc. In other words the substance of the book is the book itself—its very material evidence. Yes, that is what *we* mean by the use of the word substance. But that is *not* the meaning of the word as used here in the text. The word used is in Greek, *hupostasis*. It is made of two words: *hupo*—under, and *histemi*—stand. It is that which *stands under*. It is *not* the object hoped for, but that which stands under and supports that object in bringing it into material manifestation. If it were the object, we would need no faith, for we would have the desire. *"For what a man seeth, why doth he yet hope for?"* (Rom. 8:24). Faith cannot mean the material substance, for that would be a contradiction and utter foolishness.

Faith is like my arm which reaches out and supports or stands under the book or object I am bringing down from the shelf. My arm is not the substance or object, but is the *stand-under* which supports the object in bringing it down. Here is a definition of faith by Vaughn which I like very much because it gives us the true conception or meaning of the word.

"Faith is that principle, that exercise of mind and soul, which has for its object things not seen but hoped for, and instead of sinking under them as too ponderous, whether from their difficulty or from their uncertainty, stands firm under them—supports and sustains their pressure—in other words, is assured of, confides in and relies on them."

This should be a word of comfort and encouragement to those who are trying to fool themselves into believing they *have the object* of their faith when they have only faith. I have seen many of God's children struggling to make themselves believe what God does not ask nor faith demand. They think that if they had faith they would have the very object and material substance of the thing. You cannot have both. Faith first, and that brings you the material substance. They think they have no faith and so go down in a bog of unbelief and doubt and fear. God does not want you to say you have the material thing when you haven't. He does like us to declare our faith and say we have *hupostasis* or the stand-under which brings the object to materialization. So do not try any more to make faith mean something which it *does not, but know that all God wants* of us is to exercise our *hupostasis* which is bringing to pass the things hoped for. We stand and praise God while *hupostasis* brings the things to pass. Faith is not a struggle, it is a rest and a support—it stands under.

I like to think of Abraham. *"He staggered not at the promise of God through unbelief but was strong in faith, giving glory to God."* (Rom. 4:20). The word *staggered* is what unbelief and fear make us do—we stagger. But faith, *hupostasis,* supports and holds the conditions up for us. Why didn't he stagger? Because he had faith— not the material thing as yet. That is what we mean when we say, "We have it by faith." I know this term is abused and is often made an excuse for unbelief. How- ever, there is a truth in it. We mean that faith is opera- tive and though the material manifestation is not yet seen, the thing is moving on to its material accomplishment. So it is as good as done and we can *call those things which be not as though they were.* Faith is like a check to be cashed at a bank where the actual money is. The check is not the actual currency or gold, but it is equal to it and stands under until you get the money in your hand. Then the check is not needed—the money is all one needs.

Now let us consider the word *evidence*. The R. V. (Margin) puts it, *the proving* or *testing*. Many seem to think because faith has to do with the unseen and immaterial things of life that there is no such thing as evidence in the matter. They think faith has to do with some uncertain element in the universe. Here is where they are mistaken. The very foundation upon which the assurance and conviction rest is the Word of God. When we have faith, we take God at His word and believe what He says. Faith is not belief without evidence. It is belief on the very best and surest of evidence, the Word of God, who cannot lie.

As an illustration of having faith in His Word, let us consider Peter walking upon the water. In Matt. 14: 22-33 we have the record. *"And straightway Jesus constrained His disciples to get into a ship, and to go before Him."* v. 22. They are in divine order and acting in obedience. However, a storm comes upon them. Trouble or oppositon may not truly indicate one is out of order, backslidden or in disobedience. Very often we find a severe test may prove one is in divine order for the sake of discipline, development of faith and spiritual culture.

Verse 27. When Jesus finds them in trouble, He does not rebuke them, but gives them a word of cheer and comfort.

Verse 28. Note the reaction on the part of Peter, *"And Peter answered him and said, Lord, if it be thou, bid me come unto thee on the water."*

This is so artless, unstudied, spontaneous and refreshing—just like Peter. This venturesome spirit seemed to please the Master. He does not say: "Why Peter, what good would that do?" He sees more than Peter's desire to be near Him. He sees an occasion to prove faith and develop Peter.

In verse 29 we have *evidence* needed. The word *Come*, spoken by Jesus is the key to the situation.

"And when Peter was come down out of the ship, he walked on the water."—Upon what did Peter walk? All will say, "Upon the water." Yes, true as far as the physical was concerned. But *more*. He walked upon "Come." That word from Jesus was all he needed. He in faith laid hold of "Come," and he had all the divine evidence needed. He was safe and could dare to boldly venture out upon the water. He was walking upon the eternal Word—nothing could be safer.

In verse 30 we find the effect of recognizing natural conditions in the realm of the spiritual and region of faith. Fear enters and disorganizes the whole scene—Peter begins to sink.

In verse 31 note the exquisite grace and tact of Jesus in dealing with Peter, *"Immediately Jesus stretched forth his hand."* Help comes first, the rebuke later. As He holds Peter, He rebukes him. The safe place for a rebuke is in the arms of the Lord. He can hold while He rebukes or corrects. I think were it not so, some of us might run away from Him in greater fear.

In verse 33, note the results of this incident. Peter actually walked on the water (a miracle for Peter) and he learned a lesson in faith. And the Lord received worship. Many might think this an unwise and uncalled-for display, but when two beautiful features are forthcoming I am glad Peter ventured.

Now a word as to evidence again. The evidence remember, is His Word. But this does not mean we have a right to pick here and there the promises which suit *our* desire and try thus to make faith bring things to pass. Note that Peter did not venture until he had the word from the Lord

—"Come." He did not just venture out, thinking because Jesus was there all would be well. He got His word *first*.

In Matt. 8:23 we have the story of another storm and the disciples in a boat. But there is a difference. *"And when he was entered into a ship, his disciples followed him."* I wonder sometimes if we do not venture into realms or enter into conditions for which we have no spiritual capacity or equipment and often find the situation too great in its demands for our limited faith and experience. Let us tread softly—not fearfully, not in a spirit of presumption and credulity rather than faith (based on *His* word).

Many Christians are upset in their faith because they venture out upon a word or promise from the Bible thinking they have a right to risk all upon it—when in truth the verse of promise may have no application to the situation at all. And because God does not answer they are thrown into confusion and doubt. Many times the human heart is governed by motives and desires not in line with God's purpose or plan and so one needs to be careful to let Him search the heart in this regard.

One may be moved by personal desires, a set of spirit, a desire to defend God's glory, or maintain His honor, and be so determined to have what *he* may call victory that he battles in faith until exhausted. But that does not mean God has guaranteed or is bound by any oath to answer the prayer. The human heart is subtle and deceitful, and the motives prompting prayer should be suggested by the Spirit, born of God, and then faith can and does lay hold to victory.

Do not venture upon the water without a divine "Come" under your feet. (Do not get into bondage now and not venture at all!) But do please His heart by listening to *His* word to you and then act upon it. There are plenty of

His words for us to venture upon and as we do so we grow in faith and please His heart.

These are testing days and an age of mechanical, industrial, and material encroachment, yet we look not at the things seen but away unto Jesus the Author and Finisher of our faith.

OUT OF THE STRONG

U p from the vineyards of Timnath
   A young lion came one day—
The flesh in its strength and beauty—
   And roared as he sought his prey.
Snarling and growling from hunger
   He moved down life's dusty road,
And roared as he saw a Christian
   Alone and near no abode.

The Christian stood without weapons,
   No carnal strength did he know,
But clothed with Jehovah's power
   He fearlessly met the foe.
The Lion of flesh then gathered
   All powers that he could bid,
But the Spirit was triumphant
   And rent him as though a kid.

A helpless heap by the roadside
   The vanquished young lion lay;
Under the hot, eastern sunshine
   His beauty turned to decay.
His roar became but an echo
   The Christian at times could hear
As he journeyed on to Timnath—
   God's love casting out all fear.

The sun continued its shining;
  The flesh all rotted away
Exposing a dried-out carcass
  Where the honey bees came to stay.
Bees make no honey in lions
  That roar in the flesh and cry,
Nor still in dead lions rotting,
  But in carcasses bleached and dry.

Often returning from Timnath,
  The Christian now homeward bound,
Turns off from the dusty roadside
  Where a place of spoil is found,
And humbly gathers sweetness
  Where his roaring flesh once died,
Enough for himself and others
  From a carcass bleached and dried.

—John Wright Follette

15.

SAMSON SLAYS A LION

For our lesson this afternoon I want to bring to our remembrance an Old Testament story, familiar, I am sure, to all of us. I trust there shall be conviction and also inspiration and help in the analogy we may draw from a dramatic incident in Samson's life. I wish to talk about Samson and the lion he slew. The story is recorded in Judges, fourteenth chapter.

First, let us notice that the slaying of the lion is not the main objective toward which Samson is moving. It is rather an experience he encounters as he travels toward his objective—Timnath and a wife. One may be helped here. Do not interpret any single experience in the Christian life as final. No one experience, no matter how graphic, arresting and profoundly moving it may be, should be counted as the final objective of Christian living. Life is made up of a series of crises and telling experiences, but all are in turn to lead one to a more comprehensive understanding of, and spiritual approach to the consummation.

Samson is looking toward and desiring to reach Timnath and a wife. The meaning of the word *Timnath* is possession, or inheritance. And is that not just what every wide-awake, spiritually-minded Christian is seeking? To receive Christ as a personal Saviour and the mighty Baptism of the Spirit and the gifts, are all initial and make an equipment, as it were, with which to move out by faith and so actually *possess* what Christ has freely given us, and what the Holy Spirit longs to lead us all into.

"He that spared not his own Son, but delivered him up for us all, how shall he not with him also freely give us all things" (Rom. 8:32)! Is that not wonderful? It is revolutionizing to receive Christ as a gift, but the text says that *with* Him we are *also* to receive *all* things that come with Him—the possession for Christian living. In the normal life of man, the wife is the complement or completing factor. The full meaning and significance of the normal life as planned by God is in this plan and union. So in the normal life of the Christian, the complete, normal and perfect life is one made up of proper adjustment and understanding between the *natural* expression demonstrated in the physical life *and* the correct meaning and use of the *spiritual* significance of life.

I cannot take time here to develop this glorious, spiritual truth, as suggested by Christ Himself, in the answer He gave Satan when tempted in the realm of the natural: *"Man shall not live by bread alone, but by every word that proceedeth out of the mouth of God"* (*Matt.* 4:4). Here Christ is taking the place of the ideal man, or the last Adam and as such, makes a difference between the sources of life and power. Even as man (the perfect thought of God) the *first* suggestion is *above* the natural to God; He does not say Christ or angels, but *man* is not to live by bread alone. In other words, the normal, properly adjusted life of the person is not only human and material, but there is the spiritual side to be cultivated and trained to make a perfect balance in living. He is to live first by a spiritual touch and communion with God, the vital and supreme source of all life.

So Samson has come to a great awakening—he desires Timnath and a wife. But you must remember that the *desire* is one thing and the possession quite another. The desire moves on to a stage of faith and great adventure, and he starts down the dusty road toward Timnath.

Next in order is the lion—very true to life. And what is the lion? you ask. One does not need to press very far toward possessing his rights in Christ before he finds who or what the lion is. It is nothing less than the flesh or nature which always resists and opposes the Spirit and hinders any approach toward spiritual possessions.

The Scripture says it was a *young* lion. This is very suggestive indeed. It is not an old, worn-out lion with teeth gone and nearsighted. He is young, agile, strong and beautiful. His skin is soft and tawny, his limbs are nimble and sure as he moves along—a picture of grace and beauty. Is he not the king of beasts? What a picture of the natural man, the human heart! We are quite mistaken if we restrict the meaning of the word *flesh* to ugly, outbreaking forms of sin such as murder, pride, adultery and selfishness. The word *flesh* in the New Testament is *sarx,* and means the whole natural man—his fine and splendid powers for natural expression, his gifts in the realm of nature, his good, *religious* desires and commendable features are *all* natural—*sarx* or flesh.

As we have moved on with God into deeper fellowship I am sure we have discovered this truth. The word *flesh,* when used in the Bible with a moral meaning, refers not only to the physical body, but means the whole of the unregenerated person—spirit, soul and body. The life impulses and desires are called "lusts of the flesh." "*If by the Spirit ye are walking, ye shall not fulfill the lusts of the flesh*" (*Gal.* 5:16). Also see Eph. 2:3; 2 Peter 2:8; Rom. 13:14; 1 John 2:16.

Note that the Bible use of the word *lust* is not restricted to inordinate desires, for the Holy Spirit is said to *lust against the flesh.* Gal. 5:17, also Jas. 4:5. The word *flesh* does not necessarily mean anything vile and vulgar. The Bible speaks of *fleshly wisdom, fleshly tables of the heart, fleshly mind.* Paul does not say his body or nature alone is fleshly. He says, *"I am fleshly"* (Rom. 7:14), and also *"in me (in my flesh,* sarx) *dwelleth no good thing." Flesh* is self. In other words, anything in my natural make-up or disposition which opposes the Spirit and the development of spiritual life, is flesh. How beautiful and attractive the young lion is at times. But alas! He wars, and is hungry and seeks his prey. A Christian does not have to move far down the dusty road *toward* Timnath before he hears the roar and is conscious of the presence of the young lion. Flesh and spirit are diametrically opposed and shall ever be so.

Let us now consider another bit of truth suggested by the story. Samson knew the wife was in Timnath and also that there were vineyards of refreshing grapes there, but he also knew he did not actually, experimentally possess them. He desired and anticipated both. Many Christians forget that truth is both objective and subjective. One may contemplate and be blest while meditating upon and refreshing his heart with objective aspects of truth—what we sometimes call judicial truth. But there is the subjective side also—how much of the truth so refreshing in contemplation is actually by experience, ours? One may sing himself into a glorious, ecstatic state of bliss, singing about a starry crown and white robes, but *how much* of the spiritual quality of life does he *now* possess which in turn will make the crown a real possession? Samson might have become quite enthusiastic saying, "Isn't it all wonderful! I have a wife in Timnath!" "Oh, how delightful are the grapes and how refreshing!" And all the time he is clean *this* side of Timnath, and a lion between. It is very inspiring to sing, "I am walking in the light," but are we sure our feet are not stuck in the mud?

Samson has a great, noble desire, but that young lion says, "No!" Samson is alone and has no carnal weapons. You see he did not start out to slay a lion; he *thought* he was going right down to Timnath. And is it not just so in the Christian life? The vision (when we are in the Spirit) is so real, so glorious and so overwhelming that we never think of a battle—we are too blest for that. All we think about is the lovely presence of the adorable Christ. And how good God is to let us move down the road *alone* and without natural help. How jealous God is over His own! He so desires to develop and make His people spiritual and strong. He purposely takes away the helps and crutches just to get us alone on the roadway.

There are times and certain crises when each soul must stand alone, naked and stripped before his or her lion. God so orders our steps. Were it otherwise, our flesh would call to our help all our friends, neighbors, and saints. There are times, of course, when God uses friends to counsel and help and pray for us, but in time, the very helps and crutches which served so beautifully once, only clutter the way and become dangerous to one who is called to walk by faith alone. Do not be afraid when God directs the traffic. He will send the help which you think you simply must have, off on another road, and send you down the road alone. Why? To bless you and to help you meet your lion.

Oh, yes, I know you are saved, sanctified and baptized and have the gifts—but remember, you have a lion also. And, listen, because Samson was alone no one else ever saw his lion. And if you stay alone with God when He directs your steps, no one will see your lion either. Now isn't that grand? Let us say, "*Amen!*" The Lord knows, and so do you and I, that we all have lions, but He does not ask us to lead them around in a circus parade.

No doubt many of them are evident enough without our doing that.

So Samson stands there, without a weapon or anyone to call upon, facing this great issue in his heart and life. He meets *his* lion and no one else's. Perhaps the same issue or question some of you are facing today in your desire for a deeper fellowship and richer possession. In the walk of the Spirit, let us remember the greatest problem (or enemy) is not, "Where will I get the next month's rent?" "How shall I make the next payment on the car?" Your greatest enemy or lion is nearer and far more intimate than that. God will force you into a place where you will stand alone in the dusty road of life, conscious of one fact: that none other than you yourself is causing the greatest difficulty. Stop placing the blame on everyone else and everything under the sun; you are your greatest enemy. I personally fear myself more than the devil. The devil is already conquered—but, are all the finer, subtle points of my strange personality conquered?

Then we read that the Spirit of the Lord came upon Samson and under the inspiration and power of that Spirit, he laid hold of the lion and rent it as though it were a kid, with a grace and power that startled even himself. For he well knew that he could not have done it. You will find that, over and over again this truth is taught in both Old and New Testaments, by Christ, and also by Paul, who elaborates on the teachings of Christ. The conflict is always a conflict between Spirit and flesh—not flesh and flesh. *"The Spirit warreth against the flesh and the flesh against the Spirit."* Does Christ not ask, *"How can Satan cast out Satan?"*

Here is a rich field, dealing with methods and principles and a basic theme for Christian living. Flesh cannot kill flesh. Were it not so pathetic, it would be amusing to

see, in some assemblies, the flesh trying to kill and overcome other flesh. All flesh, but of different types. I wish
we might learn the lesson of letting God by the Spirit
do what we so many times in the energy of religious flesh
try so hard to do. God says, *"Stand still and see the salvation of the Lord."* So many times the Christian becomes
overanxious (in the standing still period) and then starts
a salvation all his own. The self-reformation, by self-will
and resolutions, makes a make-shift salvation which in
turn comes clattering down over our heads.

God does not want us to depend on any powers of the
human or natural man, lest we partake of them. He says,
"Let me get hold of *you* and I can take care of the lion.
I can roar through you and slay it." You see, when one
uses any other method than God's way, the lion resurrects
all the time. One may put up a stiff battle and fight and
"the fur may fly," but after the battle the lion gets up
again, shakes himself, and starts roaring. But don't miss
the point—Samson did not stand off on the side of the
road and look on; he was most wonderfully exercised and
much occupied. He became clothed upon with the Spirit
and thus he was empowered. It took both—he became the
instrument—a divine intervention.

What does Samson do with the slain lion? He pushes
it off on the side of the road and goes on to Timnath
and the wife. This is his real business and he attends to
it. What a very sensible and spiritual thing to do! But
do not think that is the end of the story, or the one and
only lion. This lion is representative. He stands for all
the lions of the natural man. Most people have found
there is a regular menagerie—enough for all the zoos in
the country!

And now for a word of encouragement. What happened
to Samson's lion is *truth* and happens to *all* the other lion
manifestations. Remember that judicially, objectively, the

whole old lion (tail, claws and all) is dead right now. The Scripture tells us so: Col. 2:20; 3:3; Gal. 2:20; 6:14; 5:24. This is true in experience as far as we by faith *reckon, yield, mortify* (count to be dead), *put off, put away, deny self, abide, walk in the Spirit, etc.* We do not fight; we reckon.

What a glorious and liberating truth! Paul found it and lived in the power of it—and I am sure he knew a lion when he met one. Gain the victory and *go on*. So many times I have told my students, "Never let the glory of the present victory so dazzle your eyes that you cannot see the conflict or battle just down the road." Just as sure as you slay one lion there will be its mate and all the little cubs. I know, as all of us do, there is a crisis in experience when, up to all the light we have, we say an eternal *No* to flesh and nature, and, as it were, slay the lion and really consent in our wills, to its death. God takes us at our word and proves us by letting us meet as many lions as He sees good to let out. So do we show our surrender to God and He clothes us with His Spirit and gains the victory. Let us remember what Samson did— he put the dead lion off the road and *left it* alone. Will you please try to remember to do that?

Right here let me speak of several groups of people suggested by this story. First, there are Christians who seem to know nothing about the lion or possession with Christ at all. They seem to park on salvation, the baptism, healing or some wonderful experience, and stay put. They no doubt will land in heaven (for we are not doubting their salvation) yet they are weak and have little to offer that is vital and helpful. But if they once really dared to make a move toward their spiritual possessions I am sure they would discover a lion too. He is now taking a nap and not bothering them. Since they have no special conflict with the lion of greed, pride, or lust, they are deceived into thinking they are all finished and now ready for translation.

But you see, the lion of flesh may be in the subtle, undreamed-of, latent powers of the human heart, never yet given a chance to come out. Jeremiah gives a good description of the lion. Jeremiah 17:9, in the Hebrew, reads, *"The heart is deceitful above all things and it is desperately sick."* Some render it—*incurable*. A very good picture of the lion. This first group of people are often sweet and lovely but sort of useless and uninteresting.

Then we have a group who are very conscious of their possessions, of the wife at Timnath and the vineyards. They are in a continual, energetic struggle to possess these— in an eternal warfare, always in some kind of conflict, having a time of it with the world, the flesh and the devil. Their general theme, testimony, prayer and life, revolve about one matter—the flesh and overcoming: "This is flesh"; "that is flesh"; "he is in the flesh," and "that was *so* of the flesh," etc. They have become so involved in the conflict, they forget the Spirit is to do the warring; they war and roar and take on in general, until, should you see them in the conflict, tumbling around on the floor "doing conflict," you could scarcely tell the lion from the person. The dust is thick and one hears groans and a desperate prayer for possessions. But I am sure Samson did not fight all day. There is an end to all things. He got through (and with grace) and so do we.

Often in assemblies, we find still another group. These have slain the lion and now see him in death. Their theme is death, *death,* DEATH. I am dead, you are dead, he is dead, we are dead. Yea! all are now dead. The atmosphere is that of a graveyard or a morgue. I can't do this or the other, for I am dead. I must die, you must die, he must die. Please remember, that by-and-by dead things smell, and if you are not careful the whole atmosphere will tell it too. You see, these people have discovered a phase of truth very real and true, but have developed a sort of complex in the matter and have failed to know the life and resurrection to follow. Truth is balanced and often there are different phases to even one truth.

But praise God, there is another group, and I trust we may all be found in it. They do as Samson did. When he pushed the lion off to the side of the road, instead of watching it, or commenting on it, or poking it, or feeling sorry for it, he went about his business, which was Timnath and a wife. He became occupied with his inheritance, and not the lion. The wife and Timnath hold his interest and not the conflict or dead lion. I can almost hear him, "Even though I have met this lion along the way and slain him, my objective is Timnath and a wife—not this lion." He has awakened to a very vital and powerful truth. Always keep your objective before you and in correct perspective to all else in the landscape.

A man driving his car in traffic along the highway recently, suddenly discovered that all the cars ahead of him were turning right into a dirt road. He thought, of course, there was a *detour* ahead and so followed the traffic. After driving for some miles he hailed a farmer and asked, "Where does this detour end?" "Aw! this ain't no detour," replied the farmer. "You are following a funeral procession to a cemetery."

Make your own application and draw your own conclusion. Where are *you* going? So many, although they do not know it, are really following some funeral procession to the cemetery. Just to think you are getting somewhere is not enough. You are, but where? Many are in the cemetery and parked there, for they never kept their objective before them.

Of course the rotting is a very necessary part of the process in preparing the carcass—it must be clean, dry, and merely *suggest* the lion. We slay the lion and *leave* him. One is not terrified if the lion wiggles its tail or if it rolls its eyes. Samson knew the philosophy of the matter and left it alone, even though the lion switched its tail and groaned. He is dead.

Some do not seem to know or understand this truth. They are all at sea if the lion snorts or rolls its eyes in death. Can't you hear them? "Do you suppose I got the right kind of experience? I wonder if I am really saved? Was that the Baptism or some sort of emotional experience? Dear, dear, where am I anyway? What is this experience all about? Shall I tell anyone, or will he think I am backslidden? Yes, I am sure the lion wiggled his tail! Can he really be dead?" Yes, the lion is really *dead*. But if you fool around looking at him and poking him to see how dead he is, you will surely lose out. *Reckon* and go on to Timnath. The lion likes all the attention and pity you can give him, and will hold you as long as you are willing to reason. Don't *reason*—just reckon!

Shall we ever learn this lesson? Let the penetrating rays of the sun do the work and the sun will dry out the carcass. Do not be so occupied with the process; the sun completes it. There is a subtle danger in hanging around the thing—the pretty fur and fine form may arouse your sympathy and you will enter into a compromise and spoil the whole thing.

So Samson goes on and enters into his inheritance, his possessions—wife, vineyards, and Timnath. Now let us follow him as he makes a return trip to visit his old home. It is so in the life of the Christian. Walking along the dusty highway he becomes conscious of the past victories and he remembers the days of conflict and teaching. He is reviewing some of the precious lessons of faith which God taught him as he pressed on to Timnath. He thinks again of the love, mercy, patience, grace and faithfulness of God in dealing with him and his life. How wonderful is this adorable Lord as he goes over some of the lessons of reckoning, faith and identification—all so necessary to spiritual life and culture. Suddenly he comes to the very spot where one great battle took place—even the slaying of the lion. Yes, he is where he *learned* to *stand still* and let God do the roaring. He just had to, for there was no other way. How clearly now he sees he is not the lion—he is a new creature in Christ Jesus. He is not the old Adam he once thought he was, struggling to make him look and act like God's last Adam. No, he is a *new* man and he now reckons, has faith and counts and does not trust his feelings.

Suddenly he sees something along the side of the road, off near the brush—a dry, clean, weather-beaten carcass. Yes, that is all that is left of the lion—that strong, beautiful lion. No struggle, no stench, no lion! He finds but the suggestion of a lion. It is like the echo of a voice—but not the voice.

And as he looks at it, he hears in the warm, sunny air the sound of bees, humming and buzzing as they pass and repass, going and coming. He is interested and notices that they come and go to and from the carcass. Down he gets upon his knees (an excellent place for discovery) and there, hidden in the depths of the carcass is honey— sweet, lucious honey. He tastes it and finds it is most refreshing.

Is this not true to type? It is the spiritual experience of those who go on, and on and on with God. Not only does one slay a lion and move on to Timnath, but he also learns to gather honey from the conflict. Does the Word not say, *"Nay, in all things, we are more than conquerors through him that loved us"?* Praise God, that is true! He has become a partaker *first,* of the fruit. To slay the lion is to conquer, but to gather the honey from the dry carcass is to be more than conqueror. Hallelujah!

Samson does not enjoy the honey alone—the life of the truly spiritual Christian is not self-centered. Out of the abundance of a life and heart (which for necessary delays often seems to be self-centered) there flow power and life and food for hungry hearts. He has some for his mother and father and friends. And when they ask him where he got it, he does not tell them. That is his secret with the Lord. The heart knows, and God knows and that is enough. There is a lovely spiritual truth suggested in the fact that there was plenty for the household. The secret of its power and source is in the heart of the one who is exercised and moved upon by God. Remember that in the miracle of turning the water into wine, the same truth is found. When the ruler of the feast had tasted the water that was made wine he knew not whence it was! But the servants which drew the water knew. I like that, for I believe it is a bit of revelation as to the source of spiritual ministry. It is only those who serve who know; and when you truly, or spiritually serve, you will also know.

"But what are the bees?" someone asks. I believe they are the secret desires and purposes of the Lord for one who is to slay a lion. They are tokens of God, centered in the very thing that has caused you so much trouble, the thing over which you have gained the victory. He will make that very lion a place of witness—that out of it you may have fruitage. But remember, the bees never made any honey in the lion while he roared. It was too busy roaring. The bees of God's desire for fruitage never come in a carcass while the flesh is rotting. But when it is dry, clean, bleached and weather-beaten, He says, "Now, bees, you may go in."

Are you discouraged today? Are some of you still roaring? Are you saying, "It doesn't seem as if I shall ever get any honey out of this lion"? Let me tell you something: Every one of you has reached into the carcass of some lion and taken out of it *some* sweet, I am sure. And as we move on with God He will make it still more possible.

So many times in the lives of Christians (and especially workers) there is a lack of real spiritual ministry and *food* because the dear souls have no message. They have an experience but no message that is vital, fruit-bearing and helpful—no honey. They cannot wait and pay the price of rotting and dying. They think it is too self-centered and not active enough. So not only do they miss much, but their ministry is hampered or light because they have not learned this precious, costly truth. So many are trying to gather honey when the lion is roaring or when they are slaying it. Or being over-anxious to teach and preach, they reach in their hands, only to find the lion is rotting and there are no bees, and of course no honey. The carcass becomes even weather-beaten. I like that so much—it is so true.

Trust God to make every lion the nesting place for His bees, and with *joy* (a secret and sacred joy) you will reach in and gather the honey. God is with you for this very thing—trust Him and sing!

16

EMPTIED FROM VESSEL TO VESSEL

"Moab hath been at ease from his youth, and he hath settled on his lees, and hath not been emptied from vessel to vessel, neither hath he gone into captivity; therefore his taste remained in him, and his scent is not changed." (*Jer.* 48:11).

I N the text before us we find a partial statement of the judgment against Moab. It is not my purpose to take up this judgment and from an historical standpoint show the reason for and outcome of it. But I would like to take from this verse a little group of words, really a figure of speech, and find if there be any spiritual application therein for our profit.

The words, *emptied from vessel to vessel,* are so suggestive! The Holy Spirit in making use of such an expression means more than we may think from a surface or careless reading. The figure has to do with wine-making. It tells one of the methods used in producing a clear, rich, well-refined wine. It is poured into a vessel and allowed to stand for a certain length of time under respective circumstances perhaps of heat, cold, light or darkness. Then it is poured again into another. Each time there is a settling of sediment and dregs which remain in the vessel as the wine-maker carefully pours the precious liquid into still another one. This process he repeats until the wine is perfectly refined and as it is poured in clear smooth streams, it yields a freshness of scent or fragrance very choice and pleasing to the maker. This is not so if the wine is allowed to stand all the time in one vessel. If so, it *settles upon its lees* and becomes scented with the essence of the dregs and loses its proper color value.

Does not such a figure speak? We are, as Christians, familiar enough with God's methods in soul training to recognize at once its teaching. There is a very useful lesson in Scripture in which we are mentioned as vessels. The Holy Spirit uses that type to teach us lessons concerning character building, frailty, usefulness, emptiness, and other helpful truths. But the figure here is quite different; instead of being represented as vessels we are to play the part of wine which is emptied or poured out. The vessels then are quite distinct from us and are produced by the wine-maker alone and serve only for refining the wine.

I wish we could see more clearly than we do and recognize the fact that we are at the present time in the wonderful school of the Holy Ghost. God is a Master-teacher and has us, His children, in training. We are not saved, sanctified and baptized in the Holy Spirit because we are matured or a finished product. These marvelous blessings have come to us because we are not matured. So as we yield to their purposes and ends, the Holy Spirit will see to it that we are taken step by step (vessel by vessel) into growth and maturity. And with wills yielded and spirits mellowed and broken we shall then become *wine on the lees well refined*.

It is here we find one of the methods God uses in accomplishing the desire of His heart. What may that desire be? That we may be conformed to the image of His dear Son. This is a work indeed. When once we get a vision of what we are by nature and realize it is God's purpose to transform us into the image of Christ, we are amazed. Well we may be, for there is no natural power to carry out so titanic an undertaking. We are helpless before it and see that if ever it is done the power must come from a source other than ourselves. So it does. We are God's little children. *He* furnishes the means and power for our transformation. He simply asks for yielded, willing material upon which to work. Can we not afford Him this today?

Have we not all found ourselves being emptied from one vessel to another in God's ceaseless dealings? What may these vessels be? I think they represent the various trails, unique arangement of trying circumstances, peculiar conditions, unexplainable leadings, tests in relation to healing and the general array of experiences and vicissitudes common in the life of a consecrated Christian. He does not say the vessels are all alike. That would spoil the teaching given in the figure.

The vessels are quite different—scarcely two alike in the whole number. Let us consider a few. Here is one made of glass (but it is not wine colored) and as the wine is emptied into it, it assumes a yellow tinge or a green or blue cast as the color of the vessel may produce. This is the *vessel of misunderstanding*. People judge the color of the wine by the color of the glass, and at once label the wine as *off color*. Then an endless course of reasons ensues as to the cause of its being thus colored and *why* such rich looking wine should suddenly take such an unusual shade. Of course the "wine" is all the time conscious of such remarks and has a prayerful time getting *settled*. For the wine must become absolutely still and stand long enough for the sediment to settle and cling to the bottom and sides of the vessel. Many keep the wine in motion trying to explain the fact that it is really all right; only the glass is colored. Thus there is a delay and longer time is needed to get clear wine. Just as it gets settled and there is a clear condition again, the Maker carefully lifts it up and pours it into another vessel. What is left behind? Praise God, a few more dregs of self-vindication and a few more shreds of the self-life.

As the wine is poured out, it beholds the new vessel, a large, round open receptacle—gray and ugly. At first there is a shrinking perhaps—for the vessel seems so unusual, so uninviting and so absolutely unlike any into which it has ever been emptied. It is so flat and open that as the wine is poured out it can no longer keep its proper course so it runs and spreads, filling the whole open vessel. This is the *vessel of public gaze*. It is where God pours us when we are to experience public humiliation and weakness. The wine cannot gather itself up and appear in any other shape. It must spread out flat and be open to public judgment and criticism. The trying light, the confusion, and scores of remarks made concerning the "spill," (as it seems to the people) altogether work a miracle. The wine becomes quiet, yielded and silent. Then it is poured out again. Clinging to the sides of the ugly, grey vessel there are dregs of pride and self-preservation; but added to the wine is a richer hue.

The next vessel is made of clay. It is not transparent and can reflect no light. It is tall and has a long, narrow neck. It matters not about the shape of the vessel, the wine is poured into it. As usual it has some difficulty in getting settled (owing to the darkness). It has some fear as to the certainty that it belongs there. But at last it yields and fills the vessel in quietness. Here it stands for hours, days and even months in shadow and darkness. At times the wine hears music and the delightful cries of those in light; but the clay affords no transparency so the wine remembers the light found in other days and simply trusts for light to shine again. This is the *vessel of long, dark trial*. The kind in which God lets us *alone* to prove us even in shadow and darkness. But lo, it works wonders in the wine. As it is again poured forth it gleams with light—faith tried and tested. Left behind are dregs of impatience, questioning and unbelief.

That is not all. Again the wine is poured off into a new vessel. This one is unusual in size and quite unique in design. The shape is most peculiar—it is full of bulges, angles, corners, dents and ridges. The wine has a hard time in finding its way into all the odd nooks and corners. People watch it and at once consider the wine is in the wrong vessel. It was never *called* to go into such a receptacle. It is a waste of time, money and energy and so the wine's leadings must have been all wrong. This is the *vessel of strange guidance*.

Let me tell you, dear friends, God's ways are *not* our ways. He does not come down with a private secretary and explain to the public all the leadings of His children. It is certainly a death to the flesh to be taken from one end of the earth to the other and not be able to satisfy their curiosity and the reasonings of the flesh. The wine, I am sure, had no real pleasure (in the natural) in finding its way into the different bulges and dents, but it had been poured and must now needs *run* and fill the vessel. I am glad that we do not have to know *why* God does everything. Neither do we have to explain to the public *why* He leads us as He does at times. As soon as the wine is settled and the lesson learned, the gentle hand of the Maker again lifts it and pours it off. How it sparkles and gleams with fresh yieldedness and obedience. Behind are dregs of distrust and fear.

We cannot take time to speak of the many, many vessels so different in character. Here is one made of such a variety of materials—nearly everything enters into its composition. It is not at all the choice of the wine. It was never even *considered* to ask how it should be formed. This one speaks of the complex arrangement of circumstances into which we are thrust when we truly are not to blame for the situation at all. It is the *vessel of everybody else's fault*. It is an awkward place to be. People fail to do their duty, or forget, or someone is not broken and yielded, or another refuses to come or go as he should. Before we know it we are involved in a predicament quite to our disapproval.

We are often willing to go through a trial or test when we are to blame or have some touch upon it, but to be dragged into a plight with which we had nothing to do and for which we are not at all to blame, is (to the flesh) a real death. But listen. Who made the vessel? God is not blaming you for the trial or its makeup. The wine had only to yield, be poured into, and fill. We need not take too much time in telling the Lord all about the size, shape, color, and texture of this vessel. He *made it*. Rather let us melt and flow.

Enough has been said concerning the vessels and what they teach. Let us now turn to another phase of truth given here. How may the wine act in being poured? In the study of my own experience and in watching others go through trials and testings, I have found three ways we may act.

First we may be poured, but with an unbroken spirit. The will is surrendered and the pouring continues, but the dear soul keeps rigid and unbroken in spirit. So doing, the object of the pouring is lost. The soul retains its own shape and does not melt so that a sediment may settle. He has truly surrendered to God "to do His will or die" and may even die doing the will of God, yet utterly fail in that he is not broken in spirit.

Did you ever try to pour out a pan of thick milk into a smaller receptacle? You know the difficulty and result. Why the result? Because the milk was *set*. There was no brokenness in it. The text tells us that because the wine was not emptied from vessel to vessel, it settled on its lees. This is a Hebrew word which means *to thicken or curdle*. How true! Some souls are so *set*, as we say, that they become curdled. The question then is not, "Am I poured?" No, we are *all* poured and emptied. The question now is, "Am I broken?" One may be poured and emptied into a hundred vessels and never learn the lesson and "break." Oh, let us break in spirit and as we are emptied out there will be less agony, pain and distress for we will with grace melt and fill the vessel quickly.

Another way is to yield to the pouring, find ourselves filling a number of different vessels and yet, just enduring it. Quietly hidden away in our spirit there is a pout. Did you not ever yield to God in a trial and really go through, too, and yet have a little pout in your spirit? You were convinced in your intellect through God's Word and past experience that the *best* thing and *safest* thing to do was to yield and go through. You yielded your will (away back at consecration) to go through. But at times you go through the test by "enduring" and all the time say (very faintly in your heart), "Yes, Lord, I am going through, but just the same I don't think it is quite fair, for You could have made it easier," etc. You consent in will but do not break in spirit. Do you not see how very possible it is to yield to do God's will and even go to the stake, and yet not break? Many are "enduring" the pouring, but never seem to learn the lesson. Let us break and let the dregs settle.

The third way is to not only surrender in will but to break in spirit and heart. This is so pleasing to God. As we break in spirit we lose our setness; our natural spirit gives way and we become pliable and run easily into the most intricate parts of the vessel. Here we are truly able to say, "Sweet will of God," "I *delight* to do thy will, O God," etc.

Now a word as to the reason for all this pouring and emptying. Surely God does not thrust us into such trying places to mock us. Since we are consecrated our lives are not our own to order them as we might and avoid many pourings. God is back of it all. He is training us. The object in emptying us from vessel to vessel is to produce a broken, yielded spirit.

Let us note a difference here. A surrendered will is one thing and a broken spirit is another. The surrender of our wills is understood as a basic, underlying principle in the consecrated Christian. This is a foundation upon which God is working. The surrender of our wills is really giving God the permission to empty and pour us. As we say "Yes" to God's will and surrender, He begins to empty and pour. This He must do in order to produce a yielded, broken spirit in us.

The second reason for pouring us out is to keep us from settling on our lees. There is such a tendency in life to want it easy. We dislike disturbances and having to do things differently from the way we have for forty years. We are afraid even to let our work be taken by another's hands. "The road of least resistance is a rut." So if we never get poured from experience to experience, the wine gets spoiled and scented with dregs. Do not be surprised if God is emptying you from a vessel in which you have been blessed for days and months or even years. Maybe you are settling on your lees. Since

He is very choice of His wine, He may wish to refine you a little more.

Another reason is to broaden us in sympathy and understanding with each other. The one who has had but little trouble in life is not a particularly helpful person. But one who has gone through a hundred and one trials, experiences, deaths, blasted hopes, shocks, and a tragedy or two and has learned his lesson—*who by reason of use has his senses exercised*—such a person is worth while. He is able to enter into the need of suffering humanity and pray it through. He can enter into perfect fellowship with a person who is in unspoken agony of spirit and pressure of trial. He is able to look beyond the frailty of flesh and, remembering we are but dust, to trust God with a sublime faith for victory and power. Do not be afraid of the process. I see such rich possibilities in it all. We long to be of service to needy mankind. Nothing can better equip us than to break in spirit and heart and so become clear, sparkling wine, rich and refreshing.

Again let me ask, why this broken spirit? O friends, need we ask why when once we have caught a vision of the adorable Bridegroom of the soul? We not only find in Him a yielded will, but, oh, the broken heart and spirit. He became limp, weak and broken until His life was *poured* out. "Crucified through weakness" is the Word. And this was the mighty God. What brokenness! Such was one of the characteristic marks of our Bridegroom.

Do we desire fellowship with Him? If we are to be united to Him we must be broken in spirit for our Bridegroom is yielded, and broken in spirit. Do you not see more of His purpose in it all? He is getting His people more loosened from the earth than ever before and making them yielded and broken for translation. I do not want to be earthbound and "settled on my lees," do you? If not, then let us yield quickly and learn our lessons. He is coming soon, and cannot translate unbroken spirits. The material must be yielded.

As an illustration of this emptying let us consider Paul. Surely as choice an instrument as he, must have known something of this method of development. I believe that in his conversion God accomplished a feat which often takes years to gain in the lives of many Christians. I think that Paul surrendered his will then. Does he not pray immediately, "Lord, what wilt thou have me to do?"

Even though Paul surrendered his will to God's will and at once began to walk in it, there remained in him a strong, natural spirit (not necessarily wicked or too rebellious). This did not give way to a mellow, broken, quiet spirit all in one minute. We find Paul poured and emptied, and emptied and poured, time and again. Was it to get him to yield his will? Never. He was emptied from vessel to vessel because he *was yielded* in will. But in all these strange and trying experiences his natural spirit was giving way—breaking and melting until at the close of his life we find in Paul a broken, mellow spirit which led him to pour out his life and that even with a secret and heavenly joy. Look at 2 Corinthians 11: 23-29.

"Are they ministers of Christ? (I speak as a fool) I am more; in labors more abundant, in stripes above measure, in prisons more frequent, in deaths oft. Of the Jews five times received I forty stripes save one. Thrice was I beaten with rods, once was I stoned, thrice I suffered shipwreck, a night and a day I have been in the deep; in journeyings often, in perils of waters, in perils of robbers, in perils by mine own countrymen, in perils by the heathen, in perils in the city, in perils in the wilderness, in perils in the sea, in perils among false

brethren; in weariness and painfulness, in watchings often, in hunger and thirst, in fastings often, in cold and nakedness. Besides those things that are without, that which cometh upon me daily, the care of all the churches."

Is this not a very real picture of being emptied from vessel to vessel? Look at Phil. 4:11:

"Not that I speak in respect of want; for I have learned, in whatsoever state I am therewith to be content."

This is an unfortunate translation, and is misleading. From the use of the word *content* we infer that Paul became indifferent to his surroundings and was satisfied to let them mount up over him while he contented himself as best he could. That is not what it teaches. The correct reading is, *in whatsoever state I am, therein to be independent.* How very different! He did not let the condition or trial overcome him, but he became master and independent of it, and thus made it to *serve* him. So whenever any angle, corner or side of the trial rose up to torment or fret him, he melted and ran into that very part and *silenced* it. He became independent of the vessel because he recognized the wine was of more value than any earthen receptacle. He made it serve to collect the dregs and sediment of his old life.

In closing we might consider how we may more gracefully be poured; how we may break and become the desired wine. First I think we are to see God. *He* is the Maker of the vessels, *He* does the pouring, and we are *His* wine. To see this will clear up many difficulties. The Lord may use the enemy and other people as instruments in forming the trials but only to accomplish His purpose. He is first. We are *His* wine and very choice. We cost Him His life and so He is particular to have the wine *refined* even to the last degree. We only leave behind the dregs of the old creation and self life.

"Behind my back I fling,
Like an unvalued thing,
My former self and ways,
And reaching forward far,
I seek the things that are
Beyond time's lagging days."

We must then depend upon the Holy Spirit who is now given to us instead of the old, set, unyielding spirit of the natural. As we yield and break in *our* spirit, the Holy Spirit becomes all we need. Ezek. 36:27. *"And I will put* my *spirit within you...."* Some day the last vessel will be filled and the last pouring finished. May it please His heart to find in us choice wine, rich, sparkling and well refined, because by His grace we have been emptied from vessel to vessel.

SINGING PLOWMAN

G od's plow struck deep within my heart
  And plowed long furrows, one by one,
Through fallow ground so hard and firm
  From early morn till set of sun.

The plow-share was eternal TRUTH
  Which tore the hidden roots in me
And turned them to the light and air
  Till self-hood lay a field set free.

I felt Him walk each furrow plowed,
  I knew He felt the briars sting,
The field was His—it was His joy,
  For lo! I heard the plowman sing.

He only plowed that He might sow,
  There must be seed to scatter wide.
And then I felt His presence near,
  He stood in silence by my side.

And so I gave Him all of me—
  My hopes, and dreams and inner throne.
All these He scattered far and near
  And left me naught to call my own.

They fell like seed in furrows deep,
  And all were buried 'neath the sod.
All that I had went down in death
  To wait the mighty breath of God.

He did not leave me then alone
  To mourn the loss of earthly things,
To be thus stripped gave greater place
  For life His radiant presence brings.

How could I grieve for heart thus plowed?
  I covet now no sweeter thing
Than wait with Him the harvest day,
  And in the meantime hear Him sing.

—John Wright Follette

17

FELLOWSHIP WITH CHRIST IN THE YOKE

THERE is a wonderful word in one of the Epistles upon which I often like to meditate. We find it in 1 Cor. 1:9. First, we notice there is a call sounding out from the heart of God to all of us as His children. We are called *from* and *unto*. Not only from the world and sin in their visible and common manifestations, but from the whole natural order and scheme of the Adamic and human limitations. The call is sounding today by the power of the Holy Spirit down in the depths of our hearts. It may take different forms but we are conscious that it is the will of God calling us (the personal individual) out from the natural and into a life of the Spirit where a certain fellowship may be developed.

It is about this *fellowship* that I wish to speak. As we ponder over the Word we are conscious of hidden possibilities and of very intimate communion and understanding with the Lord Jesus Christ. As I studied over this question of fellowship I found it was a matter of growth, and that there were phases of it which were logical and orderly. We will consider three phases and as we do so, note that the second is a sequel or outgrowth of the first, and the third, in turn, is the normal and perfect answer to the second. We must have, of course, a common basis for the fellowship. In creation we are given that capacity. We are created in the image of God. That image, in fact, is the capacity of receptivity for spiritual communion with God. We find no tracings of His image upon any other form of His workmanship. The new birth is necessary and all other subsequent experiences in order to deepen and enlarge the power of reception. One may be tempted to think the experience or crisis is the fellowship, but we make a grave mistake often in resting in the experience and not allowing it to act as a *door into* a new phase of life and fellowship. All experiences are beautiful, wonderful and uplifting; but do not park on any one of them. They are never in themselves the life or fellowship. They are but doors. They are to work out, in and through us a manifestation of the power and glory of God; to introduce us to and give us qualifications for the life. Salvation gives us an introduction, as it were, to Christ, but we must have more than an introduction. There is a merely *bowing acquaintance*. Many have that. They go to church on Sunday and bow to the Lord, but He wants us to come closer, to tarry often and to share in the interests which are upon His heart.

He wants our hearts to understand Him and desires a platform upon which He may come to break the bread and pour out the water of life, thus beginning a spiritual adjustment so that when we are released from this present *here* and *now* we will know how to move. The Lord always had such lovely long-distance vision; He never seemed to be upset with the immediate present but was continually looking beyond. Had it not been for that long-distance vision, He never would have dared to put into the hands of those trembling, weak apostles, the glorious torch of divine revelation. Do you not think that He knew they had wiggly, wobbly natures? Did He not know that Peter would lie and swear and curse? Certainly He did, but I have a God who can look at those things and yet never be fazed by them, because He saw Peter way down through the years to come, serving Him as a strong man of God. Vision and faith did that. It was because of these that He refused to be upset by the manifestation of that local, present condition. Are you *bound* by your immediate present condition? Are you interpreting your life by the things which just now touch you? If so, you are missing what He has in store for you. These present material things are only passing and effervescent. Make them serve you; get out of them everything you possibly can. I often told my students that they should try to get something out of everything that touched their lives, even the tragic experiences.

Now the very first movement to which we are introduced in connection with this fellowship, is a very normal and logical one. It came one day to the heart of Jesus to invite His disciples—and everyone throughout the whole age who desired it—to enter into it.

When He ministered He did so first and primarily to the House of Israel. But He found no receptivity there, for Israel refused the message, and when He found He couldn't minister to them He changed His tactics. He had worked His miracles, desiring to help Israel, but they refused His help. Our Lord knew that if they would not receive it somebody else would, and I have often thought of this in connection with the outpouring of the Spirit. The Lord started something wonderful but if we do not watch our step someone else will come along and walk off with the blessings and that which He planned for us. Are we aware of the full meaning of the moving of the Spirit? And do we know why the Spirit is moving here and being lifted there? Keep sensitive to God and know why He is dealing with you as He does.

When Jesus found that as a nation there was no response, He turned and did the thing that He always does. When the great mass refuse to follow, He begins to deal with the remnant. Did you know that God was a God of remnants? When Israel failed He had a remnant. When the

Church as a body fails to testify and move on with Him, He takes from her midst a remnant. He is continually sifting and sifting, and then He takes the few kernels and sifts again. Have you ever felt Him sifting you? He is after saints to bring them into His highest purpose for them. When the great masses refuse to respond to the message and have no ear to hear, He begins to sift till He can get a remnant that will listen. How many out of that great mass of five or six thousand, do you suppose, really followed Him? He had to sift continually and take out a remnant of those who would follow on in His further revelations.

Sensing the national failure He turns to the individual and says, *"Come unto me all ye that labor and are heavy laden and I will give you rest."* He so longs to have hearts and lives united with Him in the thoughts and purposes He has for them, that He turns and invites all those who are heavy laden to come unto Him. It is as if He would say, "You have walked with this burden upon you now for centuries; you have walked to the temple and you have walked home again with the same burden; you have walked to the Pharisees, to the scribes and leaders with your burden but walked home without any peace or victory in your life. Let Me tell you what to do." He doesn't say, "Come to the temple" nor does He invite them to any shrine; He doesn't invite them to any priest or philosopher, but only to Himself, for *He* is the center and supply for all that any heart may need, so He says, *"Come unto me."* By that He means to an individual personal contact with Him. This mass movement is all out of order; things don't move in great masses; His dealings are always with the individual.

Now please remember that when Jesus came He didn't come simply to bring us happiness or joy; He didn't come just to bring us rest. All of these are included in one great element which He brought and of which He knew the world was in desperate need. He came to bring life. Death reigned everywhere—spiritual death. Oh, yes, men could run and jump and sing and dance, but it was all physical. So when Jesus came He said to them, *"I have come for this purpose, that you might have life, and that you might have it more abundantly."* Not merely life enough to put a little breath in you and perhaps get you to heaven but life that will expand into an abundant display of God. We don't know very much about this abundant life. We may know something of its joy and exhilaration. But the life more abundant means something far above all that, and I fear most of us are touching only the fringes of the possibilities that this life holds.

Now here we are, strange personalities, yielded and surrendered, washed and lined up on the sin question and possessors of this marvelous life. We contact Him and the Spirit thrills us and we are conscious of that wonderful new life so that we feel we want to go out and convert the world. This new life wants to express itself and it is right that it should. It wants to go and preach and serve the Lord. If you are *really* born you have life.

Now the Lord understood all this and He knew that the first movement in this new life would be manifested in a fellowship of service for Him. He was very wise in meeting the situation and seems to say, "Now just wait a minute." But someone may say, "Wait? Why, I have peace and victory, my burden is lifted and why should I wait?"

But He bids us listen till He has finished what He was about to say, *"Come unto me all ye that labor and are heavy laden and I will give you—."* And as we look we see a yoke—yes, a yoke. And we hear Him say, *"Take my yoke upon you and learn of me."* But we say, "What do I want to do with a yoke? That great big clumsy thing to hang around my neck when I am free! No, no," and we turn away.

But if we are open to His voice we will hear Him say, "Come, wait, till I put this yoke upon you. I bore a yoke and let me say that I am not quarreling with you because you have this new life; I know you have it, but if I left you alone in the manifestation of the new life you might never know the full meaning of real fellowship with me. New life alone never brings to you the burden that I am bearing." We say, "Oh, I am willing to do anything! I want to go as a missionary and work for you." But He answers, "Yes, I know you want all of that but I wear a yoke because I am bearing a particular burden and I want you to *fellowship* with me in *service*. Remember, I have my head under the yoke and there is a bow in this yoke for you." As long as you have your head in that yoke, you will not be doing the wrong thing. All this energy that you feel, all this desire to serve, and all these gifts will run in a channel which will be effectual in glorifying God; for this yoke is *His* will and as long as you are being yoked with Him His will is being accomplished. When He stands still then you will stand still and when He pulls, you will pull; in this way you will be having fellowship in service; you will be co-workers *with* Him, not *for* Him; serving with Him because you are yoked up.

I was born on a farm and I remember we had two oxen called Punch and Judy. I learned many a lesson there. One thing I noticed was that when those two oxen were obedient to walk in the path which was directed for them, everything was all right, but just as soon as they started wanting their own way—as folk will do sometimes when they don't want to do the will of the Lord—then there was trouble. One ox would pull one way and the other ox the other way and that was a tragedy, for when night came and our man, David, who helped father on the farm, would take off that yoke, their necks would be badly rubbed. The will of their director had galled them because they refused to obey that will. Did you ever have your neck galled? If so, let me give you a little remedy. Take the ointment of the Name of the Lord and apply it as a salve to that sore neck. He says, *"My name is as ointment poured forth."*

Another thing I noticed about these oxen was that whenever they had to stop, they would look around and see some green grass that they wanted. They didn't see it as long as they were moving along and pulling together, but just as soon as they stood still they saw it and oh, they wanted it so badly! It looked so green and fresh. "Why not have it? We are just standing still." Do you know when the most severe temptations come? It is when you are standing still. When you are moving right along in the conscious presence of the Lord you do not think about the green grass; but you stand still and see if you don't get taken up with things that you never noticed before. They have been all along the road but you had been so occupied with Him that you didn't see them. But now that you are standing still your vision gets filled with other things.

So He says, "Take my yoke upon you, for my will is the most blessed thing that you can ever have." It steadies us; it holds us; it is the means of helping us bear our burden with ease. If you tied the yoke about the middle of one of these oxen and then tied him to the stoneboat, how long do you suppose that ox would go without having trouble? Suppose it were tied around its hind leg? The hind leg is strong, why not tie it there? But you know if that were done it wouldn't be long till the hind leg would be out of joint. How are you bearing the burdens that God has laid upon you? Is your leg pulled out of joint so much that you cannot walk in the Spirit anymore? If so, then you have been bearing your burden in the wrong way, "Oh," but you say, "I cannot understand what the Lord is trying to do with me. I don't seem to be getting anywhere with Him." Perhaps you have the yoke tied around your middle and you are bearing the burden in a way He never intended you should. Let the yoke be fastened about your neck. The neck stands for *submission* and when the will of God rests upon my neck I show that I am in submission, that I am working in perfect co-operation with my divine Companion.

One of the Gospels is called the *Ox Gospel*—Mark, the Gospel of Service. An ox was sometimes used as a sacrifice. You may either be a sacrifice or a servant. Can you be an ox for Him? You know when you get yoked up with Him you get so close to Him that you can get His very breath; you can see His eyes, sense the pressure and feel the pull that is upon His heart so that you are consumed with Him instead of scampering around on some hillside. It is then that your service is sanctified, and owned of Him; kept where He wants it because you are yoked up with Him.

Now all these things which He asks us to take are symbolic. Our first service for Him is always manifested in some kind of activity and when we are made partakers of His life it moves out in some manifestation of service. Then how wise He is! The instant that He finds our love going out in service He says, "Now wait a minute! Get yoked up with Me and you will be safe." Otherwise that manifestation will get us nowhere; it may be a display but there will be no fruitage.

Now the next thing after He mentions the yoke, He says, *"Learn of me, for I am meek and lowly of heart, and ye shall find rest unto your souls."* He has already given us the rest; that is an immediate possession—a gift. But having given the rest He wants us to learn of Him. Learn what? You say, "I am all right." No, we are but babes in Christ, little inquiring babes. Now little babes can be saved and sanctified and baptized and have gifts; all of this is not a sign of maturity. He wouldn't even give them to us, excepting, that in their reaction they mature us. Remember, it is never a sign that we are deeply spiritual or wonderfully developed in God when He baptizes or gives gifts. He baptizes us because we are babes that need life and help and then upon these weak bodies He deposits the gifts of heaven.

So Jesus said, *"Take my yoke ... and learn of me."* "Learn, when we have had all these wonderful experiences?" Why, yes, bless your heart! He has only started to get you ready, to introduce you to the schoolroom. He saves, sanctifies, baptizes and gives us the gifts and then sets us down in the primary department, puts a primer in our hands and says, "Now learn to spell." And then we begin to learn all sorts of lessons in obedience, lessons which will develop us and make us mature; and then He moves us up to the second grade. Oh, I know some of you thought you were graduated and ready to sit on a throne with the Lord! What under heaven would some of us do sitting on a throne as we are now? If in the next age He should give us some divine commission which required certain elements of character, and we had not had our training here, whatever would we do? I am sure it would be a merciful thing to keep us from such a throne experience. Capacity, power, development—these are the things that will qualify us for such positions, and nothing else will ever do it.

Knowing all this, He says, *"Take My yoke ... and learn of Me."* We think we are serving Him so wonderfully when we are bearing this yoke, but let me enlighten you. He lets us think we are doing something when all the time *He* is bearing the burden and pulling the load. *"Take My yoke upon you and learn of Me."* Do you see what He is trying to say? "I will take care of the pulling, for I am doing it anyway, only you don't know it." We are to learn of Him because we are stupid and ignorant. Blest beyond words to express, but stupid and untaught.

Just one little secret in connection with this. If the burden gets too heavy and the yoke too hard to bear, there is something wrong. He says, *"My yoke is easy and My burden is light."* His yoke is His will, and the burden is that which we incur by *doing* His will. So when we find the yoke becomes uneasy and the burden too heavy it is very likely because we are doing our own will and bearing some burden which He has not laid upon us.

In this verse we find two *rests* mentioned. First, the rest which He gives in salvation—the burden of sin is lifted and the soul, worn and tired from that burden, enters into the *rest* thus mentioned. However, as we journey down life's road there will be many burdens to bear, and our hearts ofttimes will become weary. But ample provision is made, for He says, *"Ye shall find rest to your souls."* This is progressive discovery. So we find the first phase of this fellowship consists of co-operation in service with our blessed Lord. His yoke (His will) is upon us, the power of His Spirit is thrilling the heart, and life finds a proper channel for its movements. Then God's heart is satisfied, His name glorified and we enter into an understanding of His will and purpose.

18.

FELLOWSHIP IN THE CROSS
AND CROWN

AFTER our Lord Jesus Christ gets the young Christians yoked up and they are rendering beautiful service with the blessing of God upon them, when He has them so close to Him that they can look right into His eyes and they are pulling along together, He begins to deal with them on other lines than merely serving Him; for that is not the end of the program, though some may think it is. Some people have the idea that if they just serve Him till the trumpet blows they will be ready to enter in, but let me tell you that is only the beginning. Most of this service has its counterpart, symbolized by the next thing He tells them to take. They have taken the yoke and now we find, about four chapters further on, that there is still something more for them. For we find Him saying to His disciples, *"If any man will follow Me, let him deny himself, and take up his cross and follow Me."*

But we might question, "A cross, right when we are moving along down the road of wonderful victory and power? A cross?" Yes, that is the next thing He has for us. Never try to load a poor *sinner* up with a cross. He has nothing to do with it. Get him to take the yoke if possible but not the cross at first. And remember that we are not now speaking of the Cross of Calvary—that belonged to Jesus. He tells us to take *our own* cross. It is as if He said, "Now I have you exercised sufficiently and have you in good running order, and it is time for you to take up your cross and follow Me." Why does He say that? Because the cross is a symbolic term. The yoke is the symbol of service, the cross is the symbol of suffering; the crown is the sign of authority, and the palm is the symbol of victory. All of these are symbols or pictures.

The Lord is speaking of the invisible crosses which face every heart that is actually serving the Christ in this yoke life. Every bit of spiritual service issues in suffering and it is necessary that we suffer—it is a part of this cycle of which we have been speaking.

You thought the yoke was given so you could serve the Lord? It was not that *only*. It was that He might, through the medium of service, captivate you so you would then take up the cross. He could thus move you into still another phase of this fellowship. So He draws a halt to all this activity.

You thought you were pulling along beautifully, but that was only to get you started. Did you not know that what you *are* is of far more value than anything you *do?* The worker is always of more consequence to God than anything he can ever do and yet it is the work which seems to captivate thousands and thousands of Christian workers. To all such whose vision is filled with the work they do for the Lord let me say, "You have your focus wrong; the vision is all right but the focus is wrong; never focus it upon anything you do. It is *you* He wants and not so much the things you will accomplish.

He says, "If you will do that which I am asking of you, then I can not only get something done for my kingdom but I will also accomplish something in you and through this I will be able to stamp upon you a little more of the divine image until you come to the full stature of Christ." So He draws a halt to this lovely picture of service and says, "Now take up this cross. It is not Mine, but is for you alone." This does not mean that we cease to serve Him. We are now conscious of a cross and its place in our life.

But you say, "If Jesus died on the cross, why should I have a cross?" That you might do the very same thing that He did. The cross is a symbol of suffering, of crucifixion, and He wants your heart and life brought through the death process.

Being saved, sanctified, baptized and used in His service— all this is but preliminary to getting you ready to be placed upon that cross. The Paschal lamb was standing in all its perfection without spot or blemish, sanctified to the Lord, but Jehovah didn't say, "Tie that perfect lamb to the door and when the death angel passes over he will see this beautiful lamb and pass over." We are not saved by life but by *death*. Do you want to live? Then take your cross. What is your cross? You will have to learn to interpret your own cross, for yours is not like anyone's else. It will be a cross fitting your whole concept and disposition, and more than that, your *will*. Whatever you are *in your will,* determines your cross. What may be a cross to you may seem like a joy-ride to another. It is that which will crucify the *I* in you that will determine your cross; whatever sort of a cross will do away with that "straight-up-and-dicular" pronoun, will be the one He means you to take.

He has shaped it and brought it to you but He leaves the taking of it to your own volition. He doesn't lay it upon you. That would spoil it. It is the surrender of your being to the cross that He wants. Take it in faith, always re-membering that on the other side of that cross there is a further step to this cycle to which He is calling us. We have that to encourage us.

Let me admonish you—never make your own cross. How easy it is to make crosses for ourselves! I remember years ago when I first came into this teaching and the Lord, leading me out on this line of thought, began to search my heart and to crucify me. I thought sometimes I would almost perish. Sometimes the reaction of it would nearly overwhelm me and yet I told the Lord I wanted more of it; I told Him I wanted to know the philosophy of it, the meaning, even though it took my life. He created that hunger in me; it was a God-made hunger. And He began to feed me with some of these luscious things of the Spirit which come *only* by this process. I saw that I should be crucified and I endeavored in my own strength to let this crucifixion work in my heart and life. I found I was not progressing, so one day while on my knees, the Lord, as it were, leaned over me and whispered, "Now just wait a bit. I know how to make crosses. I worked in a carpenter shop and I know just how to shape them." I knew well what He meant—I was not to do any more of this self-crucifying business. You know why? Because everytime we make a cross for ourselves we always pad it somewhere with a cushion. But when you allow Him to form the cross He has a unique way of managing it all. Take up the cross He has made for you, but don't shy off. Hundreds of people have side-stepped their crosses. Oh, they will not miss heaven because of it but I know some things they *will* miss over there!

He says to us, "Deny *yourself*." Now don't start denying yourself of *things*. He doesn't ask you to do that. It is this miserable, evasive, hateful, ruinous thing in us which we are to deny. Don't you hate it? You may deny yourself of *things* till you are skin and bones and still retain that hideous thing that wants to rise up and be "It" and *say* and *do* and *have*, when instead, it should always be "Christ in you the hope of glory." I can of myself do nothing, but *I live;* as Paul says, *yet not I*—not this terrible *ego*—but *Christ liveth in me.*

When He says, "Deny *yourself*" He is striking at the

fundamental *element* again. The *I* in us is the only *thing* that wants to live in us. God knows that and is saying, "If you continue to allow that *I* to move under the power and realm of the creation in which it is born you will die a wreck." If you are unsurrendered and unsaved all you need to do to get to hell is to keep on having your own will. Don't think for a moment that you have to go out and commit adultery or lie and steal to be lost; if you keep on allowing that ruinous self-will to exert itself and remain unsurrendered to God you will land in hell.

That is why God always asks for our surrendered will. With my will I have power to attain, by the power of choice, the highest place in God or to wreck my life. God never coerces anyone. He asks us to take up our cross, to deny ourselves—deny that which wants to rule us. Every time you feel it rising up, deny it. You know when it comes. Did you ever have a secret meeting in your own heart? Do you know these movements in your heart of hearts? God knows them and He would like to have us honest enough to sit down with Him, as little broken-hearted children, and face our failures, call them by their proper names. Would it not be profitable to admit that we are miserable failures? But instead of that we begin to make excuses and say, "Well, if so-and-so had not done that it wouldn't have happened." Have any of you here ever discovered that you were not absolutely perfect after you were baptized? If you think you are a finished product you are deceived and I would far rather deal with an honest sinner than with you in that state. God wants reality. He knows that this *I* will go forty miles out of its way to make itself prominent or to spare itself. It is all a part of the colossal ruin of Adam. I have often thought that if our hearts were all hung on a washline from here to Jerusalem we wouldn't be able to pick out our own. In the natural we are all of the *same clay*.

Now Jesus says, "Being identified with Me take up your cross and follow Me." Where will you follow? He walked from Bethlehem's manger to the city of Jerusalem and lived a most wonderful life. Is that the only place where He walked? And did He go right from there to heaven? True, there is that lovely picture of the Mount of Transfiguration where Jesus stood in the perfection of manhood. But He was *more* than that. He is the Lamb that must be slain. He went down from the Mount to the demoniac of humanity at its base, and later on climbed up Calvary's hill and made His exit from Calvary.

Are you to follow this Jesus just where His miracles are being performed? That would be interesting, but you will have to be careful. He will lead you right through Gethsemane to Calvary. There is something wonderful about it all, for as you find your Gethsemane and your Calvary you will also have the fellowship of this Jesus whom you so love. You will share in the fellowship of His suffering. Remember that every bit of spiritual service issues in suffering. His service never rides in a band wagon. He has other means of locomotion. You will not amount to much on the band wagon; it may roll on for a time but by and by you will hear the wheels creaking so you had better get off and get down on the ground. The bride of Christ doesn't get to heaven on a band wagon. He has other means of locomotion. You will find it in Genesis. Remember the camel.

As we follow the Christ in His walk we find that He grew in wisdom and knowledge and in favor with God and man. From the human aspect He has the favor of men and they like Him; He was a fine young Jew. Then something happens. God leads Him to be baptized in the Spirit and through a terrific pressure He becomes partaker of that inward revelation of God the Father. God is truth and therefore this Jesus must be a revelation to the world of what truth is. He becomes the embodiment and personification of truth, insomuch that He can stand up and say, *"I am the truth."* No one else could have done that.

And the moment He declares Himself to be *truth,* the attitude of the people changes. In the synagogue where He has always been welcome and in perfect harmony with all the people, when He takes His place in the Messiah's chair and dares to say to them, *"This day is this prophecy fulfilled in your ears,"* what is the reaction? They hate Him and would have killed Him. What has happened? His personality has not changed, but He has taken it upon Himself to be identified with God in *truth,* and truth is the thing they hate. Always distinguish between the two— personality is a evasive thing, but *Truth* is dynamic. Oh, yes, the philosophers wanted to know what truth was, but when they had the very Embodiment of truth in their midst they rejected it. They would rather get it second- third- or fourth-hand; they are afraid to get too near the fire and they fear that direct truth might inconvenience them. So they seek to get rid of Truth by throwing Him over the precipice, but you cannot get rid of truth that way.

He had not really served in anointed ministry up till that time; He was simply that beautiful thirty-year-old young man. But just as soon as He begins to serve in the capacity of truth He ceases to be in favor. Listen, the ministry which does not demand a price of us is not worth anything. And it is a strange thing, but the more you embrace that truth the greater become the desire and hunger in your heart for more of it. A spiritual ministry dealing with *truth* is the most costly service.

Now why do we suffer in our service? It is in our catalogue. Any Christian who thinks suffering is not on his program has a mistaken idea. On Calvary Jesus met every other condition; He met the entire sin problem and made provision for it but He never put suffering out of the

program. He uses suffering to serve us. But don't let yourself get crushed beneath it. Suffering, if borne in the Spirit
and to the glory of God, will issue again into a new fellowship with Him; but it cannot be entered into unless you
come the way He has designed.

Now let me read from Romans 8, *"And if children, then
heirs; heirs of God and joint-heirs with Christ, if so be
that we* SUFFER *with Him that we may be also glorified
together. For I reckon that the sufferings of this present
time are not worthy to be compared with the glory which
shall be revealed in us."* We are candidates for heir-ship.
That is, it belongs to us *if so be that we suffer with Him.*
Where is He bringing us? To a place of glorification with
Him. That is our final destiny. It comes by way of the
yoke—but don't stop with the yoke; by way of the cross
but don't stop at the cross; by way of suffering but
don't stop at suffering. Move on. He wants us finally to
be glorified with Him. I love Him because that is His
divine arrangement and program.

We are all heirs, but there is a great difference between
being an heir and actually getting your possessions. Did
you think just because you were an heir you would get
it all the next afternoon at two o'clock? There is "many a
slip 'twixt the cup and the lip," you know. He says we
are candidates for heirship, and we may become joint heirs
—yoked, or joint heirs with Him, *if.* Oh, that little con-
ditional *if.* Is it on condition that you receive the Baptism? No. On condition that you are a Christian? No,
you have all that to start with but that is merely to get
you inside the schoolroom door, and puts you in the first
seat where you are looking at the letter *a.* Now you have
all the remainder of the time to study out these intricate
things of God.

Children in the primary department are heirs to all the
education of High School and University but we don't go

to them and say, "I love you so that I will just put you in High School today." Yet people think God will do that very thing. It is ridiculous. No, He says we shall be joint-heirs in that glorification, in that unveiling, in that mystical union that He had with the Father, *if* we suffer with Him. Have you learned to suffer? That strange crucifixion is to qualify you with capabilities that will make it possible for you to reign with Him.

Yes, our reigning with Him requires qualifications. I was once a teacher in public school and learned some lessons there. I have taught in all departments for we were required to take the children on up through the grades to High School. While I always had a certain amount of fellowship and understanding with every grade because I adapted myself to my pupils and loved the children, yet I learned that, with all my devotion to them and all my interest in their welfare there was one thing I could *not* do—I could not impart to them in one day, qualifications or ability to land them in the high school classes or send them to college. All I could do was to keep eternally setting before them their lessons, teaching them, coaching them so that one day they would be able to adapt themselves to their new realm. How ridiculous it would have been for me to take a child in the early grades and transplant him right into a high school class! He wouldn't know how to adapt himself.

And do you think that some day the Lord will come and take us up and then come around with a bunch of crowns and say, "Now here is your crown"? and "Here is yours"? or "Here is a pair of wings for you and a golden house"? Is that what fellowship with the Son consists of? Is that the deep spiritual understanding that you learned when you were in the yoke with Him? when your face was so close to His? when you were so close that you understood the intimations of His heart, and felt the warmth of His nature? Ah, no! It was then that you received something that *transformed* you until finally you found you were not the same creature that first went into the yoke with Him; you found yourself in perfect union and in love with this mystical Christ until you were partaking of His glory.

Do you want this fellowship with Christ? If so, it will cost you everything you possess, but it is worth it all. Let all else go; become detached and liberated from everything earthbound and move along with Him in this blessed fellowship, first in the yoke, then in the cross and its suffering and eventually you will enjoy that supreme fellowship of reigning with Him.

19.

CHRISTIAN CHARACTER—
A QUALIFICATION

WE have been considering the subject of Christian character from several viewpoints. Let us think of it as qualifying us for Christian living, and trace its importance as suggested by some scriptures I shall read. Let us consider two pictures together—one from a positive, the other from a negative point of view.

"Let us be glad and rejoice, and give honour to Him: for the marriage of the Lamb is come, and His wife hath made herself ready. And to her was granted that she should be arrayed in fine linen, clean and white: for the fine linen is the righteousness of saints." Rev. 19:7, 8.

"And when the king came in to see the guests, he saw there a man which had not on a wedding garment: and he saith unto him, Friend, how camest thou in hither not having a wedding garment? And he was speechless. Then said the king to his servants, Bind him hand and foot, and take him away, and cast him into outer darkness; there shall be weeping and gnashing of teeth. For many are called, but few are chosen." Matt. 22:11-14.

By way of suggestion, remember that the *called* are always referred to as saved people. The very word translated *church* means the called-out ones. Look up the references concerning called, calling, call, etc., and you will find they refer to saved people. Food for thought.

When we consider this subject we must at once remember the difference between the divine nature and Christian character. If we do not, there is confusion and much of the process of building life and the necessary discipline loses its significance. Only as we keep the difference in mind and see the *need* of building character are we able to interpret many of the disciplinary measures God permits to come our way.

The divine nature of which we are partakers (2 Peter 1:4), the new creation, salvation, or new life (there are several terms to express it), that experience of salvation, is a *free* gift. *God so loved the world, that He gave....* We become recipients of the new life and nature by faith in the finished work of Christ for us. We become babes in Christ by a new birth (a gift of God). We neither merit it nor can we earn, buy or work for it. We receive it as a token of His love, grace and mercy. This new life of course is not fully developed in the individual, that is why we are called babes in Christ, and must grow. There are untold possibilities latent in the new creation and it is the desire of the Holy Spirit to develop them in the personality and life of the individual. For this reason He has baptized us in the Spirit and introduced us more fully into the life of the Spirit, and by His ministry and our cooperation He can lead the yielded heart into fuller and fuller revelation of Christ and His purpose.

The desire of God and the purpose of salvation are not merely to get a man saved and land him in heaven. The man's salvation is not unto heaven. (That is given to him as a place after death). Salvation is *unto* a conformity to God, His image and likeness. Remember, heaven is a condition before it is a location. Even if you consider heaven in purely material terms, as golden streets, etc., your power to enjoy, understand, and correctly fellowship there is *first* determined by condition. The disciples were *very* concerned about a material kingdom (which was right and will eventually come) but Christ corrected them and placed the emphasis where it belonged then and now. *"The kingdom of God is within you." Luke* 17:21. Heaven is never spoken of as the *goal* of Christian living, but perfection of Christian character is, and is clearly taught by Christ. *"Be ye therefore perfect, even as your Father which is in heaven is perfect." Matt.* 5:48. Note the position of this statement in the teaching and discourse of Christ.

The work of the Spirit today is the conforming, molding and shaping of the individual into the likeness and image of God. He is after Christian character. *"For whom He did foreknow, He also did predestinate to be conformed to the image of His Son." Rom.* 8:29. *"But we all, with open face beholding as in a glass the glory of the Lord, are changed into the same image from glory to glory, even as by the Spirit of the Lord." 2 Cor.* 3:18. *"Beloved, now are we the sons of God* (new birth, salvation), *and it doth not yet appear what we shall be* (the fuller development and growth of character)." 1 John 3:2. *"Till we all come in the unity of the faith, and of the knowledge of the Son of God, unto a perfect man, unto the measure of the stature of the fulness of Christ." Eph.* 4:13.

Here is where many Christians fail, losing sight of their objective in the technique, mechanism and method of trying to attain it. They become absorbed in the process and seemingly rest there and are defeated, not because they did not *do* but they did not relate the *do* with the objective. Do not be deceived, Christian character is never given as a gift. Righteousness is imputed to us on the basis of His redemption, but never Christian character—this is the product of training, overcoming, discipline, trial, hardship, and intensive spiritual living. I cannot work and earn salvation, but I can apply myself to intelligent and spiritual living and build a character. He keeps the goal in mind (even when I fail to do so) and leads me through a thousand experiences to make *in* me a manifestation of His *life*. I cannot earn salvation, but by His grace I can *overcome* and thus become Christlike in life and character.

So let us keep this distinction in mind and not deceive ourselves by thinking because we have had certain genuine experiences, such as salvation, the Baptism in the Spirit, healing, or consecration, that any one or all can in themselves *give* us character. They are like a series of crises through which the Holy Spirit leads the hungry heart in its quest for truth. These experiences are open doors through which we pass (not one is finality). We must surrender to the *purpose* of the crisis—yield to the Holy Spirit and be *taught* and walk in the Spirit and possess our inheritance.

When we keep in mind the objective for the building of character and conforming to the likeness of God, we are able to understand more fully the movements of God in this dispensation. What He is doing in the life of the individual He is doing in His Body during this dispensation. If I hold any other goal or objective in mind, such as the establishment of His kingdom on earth, the redemption of the political chaos, "making the world safe for democracy!" or any other *fine, good, religious-sounding* scheme, I am at once confused and end in defeat. I cannot trace God in any of these schemes. They sound noble, mighty, uplifting and very religious, *but* they are *not* what God is doing just now. *"Simeon hath declared how God at the first did visit the Gentiles, to take out of them a people for His name."* *Acts* 15:14. This is the work of the Spirit in this dispensation.

Some will at once get jittery now thinking I do not believe in the salvation of souls and evangelism. Do not fear. There is a place absolutely for salvation and evangelism in the plan of this age, but He is not planning in this dispensation to redeem the world and usher in the kingdom. *Let both* (wheat and tares) *grow together until the harvest.* However, He does want the note of the evangel to sound, clear and strong, to the ends of the earth (as a witness). That us why I am a lover of all missionary work. It is so genuinely Scriptural. The evangelist is needed to bring in fresh material, new-born babes for the body—all for building. The world is *so* needy—let us be thankful for any and every agency He can bless today in bringing broken humanity to God.

God is making a man. He is building a race. Look at Eph. 4:11-13. *"And He gave some, apostles; and some, prophets; and some, evangelists; and some, pastors and teachers; for the perfecting of the saints, for the work of the ministry, for the edifying of the body of Christ: till we all come in the unity of the faith, and of the knowledge of the Son of God, unto a perfect man, unto the measure of the stature of the fulness of Christ."* Note the teaching here. The purpose is quite evident from verse 12, *"for the perfecting of the saints, for the work of the ministry, for the edifying of the body of Christ,"* etc. Here we find all the gifts to the church as named are *unto* the perfecting of the body. All move *unto* a new man. It is clearly shown that it is the perfecting and maturing of the body He is after. Perfection here, or the word perfect, does not mean sinless perfection but rather being full-grown and mature.

I know people at times are annoyed at me for bringing this phase of truth to our attention. I have noticed so many times in meetings where they were all saved and nearly all baptized, the service moves nearly always along evange-

listic lines, even when they are all saved. This is no doubt
due to tradition, custom, and *religious* habit. The dear saints
have been told that beautiful story from so many angles
they wonder if there can be anything MORE in the Bible
for them now that they are saved. This practice I am sure
is not *balanced*. Count up the meetings for the children
of God, the saints—meetings of instruction, illumination,
correction, building and *feeding*. I am very sure you do
not strike a balance. Now be honest! Do not ask me to
maintain a balance when there is none, please. Surely the
sinner needs salvation—but O the body of Christ—weak,
torn, undernourished, and so feeble!

"Is there no message for us?" so many ask me. I wish
some of you could hear the confession of *need* and the cry
for food some saints (saved and baptized for years and
fine workers too) pour into my ears. God placed a basket
on my arm and also *put something* into that basket. Then
He said, "Go out now and feed My sheep." So that is all
I hope to do—*share* with you truths which have taken hold
of me and revolutionized my life. My burden is for the
sheep. In my heart I can hear them cry and bleat. Why
do we find dozens of evangelists to one teacher who can
feed?

Let us turn to the text quoted from Rev. 19:7, 8. Here
we find teaching about the Second Coming—but the picture
is rather unusual. It is *so* different from the pictures usually
given when one preaches on the Second Coming. As a rule
the message revolves about the external aspect—dealing with
the national and prophetic phases, the signs of the times,
the return of the Jews, the restoration of the Roman kingdom, etc. But here we find a picture relating to His return
and touching upon the most vital point as *God* sees it.
We are called upon to rejoice and be glad. Why? Is it
because the Jews have at last all returned to Palestine?

because the Roman empire has taken more definite form? because *all* the signs at last do focus properly? No, strange to say, although all these are accompanying features—the *real feature* is, "and His wife hath made herself ready."

From this text it looks as though He will come when He has something *ready* to come for. "Be ye also *ready.*' It is a question of readiness, fitness. Look at the next verse and find *why* she was ready. In what does this fitness consist? *"And to her was granted that she should be arrayed in fine linen, clean and white: for the fine linen is the righteousness of saints."* The preparedness relates to a garment. I will read it as it is given in the Greek and as rendered in the Revised Version. *"And it was given unto her to array herself in fine linen, bright and pure, for the fine linen is the righteous acts of the saints,"* or as some translations give it, the righteous conduct of the saints.

Here is a beautiful and Scriptural illustration of the truth I am teaching. Salvation is always a *gift,* while character (a privilege granted) is a result of co-operation in building and arraying. We see at once this is *not* a garment of salvation—this is very evident. The garment of salvation was wrought out (or woven) on the loom of Calvary by Christ our Lord. *He* worked out the finished act of redemption; He made the garment of salvation. We never could. We had absolutely nothing to do with it—it was His work, noble, profound, and eternal. Amen!

In this text it says, *It was granted her*—a privilege— *to array herself*. It was something she could accept or reject— to array herself—something *she* could *do*. When we were saved it was Christ who put the garment of salvation upon us. It was Christ who made the garment and Christ who put it upon us. We stood still—poor helpless sinners. But here is a wedding garment which *we* weave. It says distinctly the linen is *the righteous acts of the saints.* No righteous act of the saint ever made a garment of salvation. It says here it is the garment of a saint. (He is not talking about sinners, but the bride). It was her readiness, fitness, preparedness, *qualifications* which gave her this *position.* She has *all* the necessary training and equipment in character to move in this capacity and to hold this lofty place. She has passed all the tests and holds the qualifications necessary for this heavenly, spiritual, holy and sacred union. She is not a stranger to the atmosphere of this place— she speaks the language of the Bridegroom. She has *learned.*

This garment speaks clearly of *preparation.* It is a process, not a gift. How does one get it? He does *not* get it by going to the altar and saying, "I will now take a wedding garment," or "I will now take a Christian character." That is quite impossible. But he may at the altar offer himself as a candidate for this lofty place and submit himself to the Spirit for the necessary discipline and training to qualify for it. Then will the Holy Spirit take him in hand and train him by way of the many experiences through which he is asked to go.

When we see this truth it helps us to RELATE (what a difficult thing) the many phases of service, the gifts, ministries, *conduct,* and LIFE as God sees them all—acting upon us. The whole scheme of life is *re*actionary. We are by creation reacting agents and God works from that point of understanding. All is *unto* the building, the arraying in fine linen(the righteous conduct of the saints).

For a moment, keeping this line of truth in mind, review the story of the talents. Matt. 25:14-30. Did you ever notice *what* the man who gave the talents really was after? Be careful here and do not clutter your picture with *all* the pounds gained—you will miss the point. It was the commendation, not the works. The works were there and necessary but *wholly for* the *reaction* found in the user of the talents. Look at verse 21. *"His lord said unto him, Well done, thou good and faithful servant."* Let us stop there now. Three commendable *character*-qualities had been wrought out in this man's life. *Well* done—not how *much* done. The quality, not quantity. Good servant—Godlike. A quality of Godlikeness is found in him. Faithful servant —another qualification. No word as to the magnitude or extent of *work*. That was all a *means* unto an *end*. The end was the training of the man.

Listen. *"Thou hast been faithful over a few things, I will make thee ruler over many things: enter thou into the joy of thy lord."* You see it was *qualification* which made that possible. He was already a servant (not a sinner). The gifts and ministries are so alluring and captivating to some souls that they forget that *all* this, even tongues, shall pass away—but the likeness and character of Christ etched upon the immortal spirit abideth forever. Amen! *The gift of salvation never qualifies a soul to reign and rule with Christ.* Crowns are not given as souvenirs—they are *won*.

So in the picture of the Bride, she hath arrayed herself, made herself ready. Surely not *for* salvation—she is already saved and wears a garment of salvation. But she is *now* able to enter into the deeper reaches of fellowship with the Son. It is not a question of God's loving one soul more than another. He is not a respecter of persons—all may qualify if the soul so desires. *It was granted unto her*— a privilege. What could thrill a soul more or stimulate love and devotion to our adorable Lord than such a glorious experience? The new creation is made for the highest heaven may offer—then why not *yield,* and let life and all go under the leading yoke of the Spirit and let Him conform us?

At once I know some are saying, "Ah! That is all too selfish, self-centered, and not as aggressive as we should be." I have heard that for years—but like Paul, "none of these things move me." In the year 1908, when God wonderfully baptized me in the Holy Spirit, He gave me understanding as to His desire and purpose along this line. And had it not been for the faithfulness of the Spirit to keep me *true* to that vision I should have been swept off my feet or completely discouraged. He keeps me under the power of the truth He gave then—*absolute* surrender, death to the old creation, the overcoming life, the spiritual life in a *new* creation, qualification for the fellowship of Christ in a new age, etc. In the meantime all my service, teaching and ministry have been means unto an end. It has mattered very, very little to me the form, *size,* and general display of the service I undertake—but the growth in the *knowledge* and *wisdom* of Christ has kept to the foreground.

It seems that only as one swings wholeheartedly into the meaning of qualifying and training is he swung *free* of the binding that too often comes with too intense and feverish attitudes of service.

God is not so concerned with *how much* we may do for Him, as He is with the question, What has all the service done to us in its reaction upon our nature and spirit? Has it all reacted in developing the man or woman into the person of faith, strength, love, and yieldedness He *so* desired to find? Did all the man did really mellow, subdue and conform that man into the new creature God wanted? According to our creation we are reacting agents and God is *wonderfully* interested at this point. *What* is all my conduct and ministry *doing* to this strange personality? It is continually registering upon my immortal spirit and weaving a garment. Shall it be a wedding garment?

Now let us turn to the story given in Matthew 22. Here is a man without a wedding garment. As a rule this story is used to represent a sinner trying to move in the realm of salvation without the garment of salvation. But let us look at it more carefully. Get the setting of the story correctly. This chapter is so important in its relation to what precedes and follows. The public ministry of Christ has covered a period of three years and in a few days He will offer His life in a sublime testimony by a vicarious death. As never before it seems He is anxious to present to His nation the offering of God's grace, mercy and *truth*. And never before has the Jewish hierarchy shown more malignant opposition. On His way to Jerusalem He speaks several parables, all of which were to show them the supreme folly of rejecting Him as their Messiah.

We must remember that the parable has a double application: First, to the Jew as a body at His first advent; second, to the church at His second advent. So often preachers and teachers and evangelists are not careful or perhaps *brave* enough to make the application *where* it belongs. Sometimes *tradition* causes it too. How often the portions of Scripture containing teaching, admonition, correction or warning for the Christian (because it is not pleasing) is turned over either to the sinner or to the Jew! The poor Jew has his plate full now of scriptures some do not know just what to do with. It is *convenient* to have the sinner around to give certain bits of Scripture which might upset *smug* theology or tradition. This picture does not relate to a sinner, as we shall see. He is giving truth for the saint—only it is not so pleasing.

Just as in the first application where we find the Jews (because of their *own* doings) made themselves unworthy of the kingdom, so at His second advent when the marriage supper is due, there are elements in the saved group who by their lack of preparation and qualification are unworthy of the fellowship and privilege offered in the picture of the marriage feast, etc. The analogy is here very clear. There are many Christians today who refuse the necessary discipline and training needed to qualify, while there are others who embrace the cross and *suffer* the loss of all things that they may *satisfy* the desire of God in getting a Bride worthy of the Son's fellowship. Note the word of the king, *Friend.* He is not talking to a sinner about his sins. He says, *Friend.* John 15:14. *Ye are my friends....* Sinners are never spoken of as friends; they are rebels. He does not rebuke or chide the man about his sins—it is rather a point of *place* or position. *How camest thou in hither?* Place, location!

The garment again speaks of character, and fitness. He had no fitness or adequate degree of fellowship and understanding to move in the sphere of a wedding feast and all that this type suggests. He had no garment—no qualifying attributes to adapt himself to the order of life suggested.

And note too he is not cast into hell, sheol, gehenna, or the pit. *Outer darkness,* is the word. Some may ask, "What is the outer darkness?" You will find Jesus using the same term in Matt. 8:12. Here it does not refer to hell, the pit or gehenna, etc. He is speaking of the lack of faith and appreciation on the part of the Jews (the children of the kingdom). And because of their refusal to accept and move into the kingdom of heaven (verse 11) they are cast out into outer darkness. Any one knows that when the Jews refused to accept Christ and the kingdom they were not cast into hell or the pit. But they were turned into outer darkness where they are today. As far as Christianity is concerned, and the kingdom Christ came to set up in the hearts of men, they are in outer darkness. They are denied (by their own choice and doing) the privilege and fellowship of the kingdom.

The term is used again by Jesus in the story of the talents and servants (*not* sinners) Matt. 25:30. The sinner has no talent or pound for which he must some day give an account. But the servant (the Christian) has. In this story the reward (verse 21) was a privilege of ruling (because he had qualified) and also the joy of the Lord. The unprofitable servant (not sinner) because he had not qualified and had NO results to show at the reckoning, was cast into outer darkness. He was not burned up but he lost the reward of ruling and the joy of the Lord. He was *excluded* from the special fellowship which he might have had had he trained and educated himself for it.

So from the teaching of Jesus, outer darkness does not mean hell or the pit but rather the LOSS and denial of a great privilege. The Jews are alive today, not in a pit, but they are in outer darkness, becaused they refused Christ. The glory and joy of the marriage feast is light. They are *excluded* from it or rejected.

"Know ye not that they which run in a race run all but one receiveth the prize? So run, that ye may obtain." 1 Cor. 9:24. (Note one does not run FOR *salvation—it* is not a prize. He runs because he is *saved* and is after a prize—the real goal.) If he is cast into the pit to be burned up, why bind him hand and foot? Here we find him in outer darkness and bound. The hands represent service. He is not *qualified* to serve in this realm. He may know service in the *natural, religious* life and service in the sphere of the flesh (natural and to some quite *wonderful*) but he does not know *spiritual* ministry—so is bound. The feet represent the walk. He may have traveled thousands of miles in the energy and power of the natural life, and fairly exhausted himself. But he does not know the "walk in the Spirit." That was always too demanding and restricting for him. He may have walked all *around* the Lord

but not *with* Him. So his feet are bound. He has *no* power to enter into such fellowship as is suggested by the picture. And alas! He might have had. What a mercy he is cast out. God is yet kind to him not to subject him to the embarrassment and confusion of face to find himself TRYING to fit in where he has absolutely no qualifications. It would not be *love* for a principal of the High School to take a fourth or fifth grade child and place him in a class of university students. That would not be love. God does no such cruel things. We are *now* qualifying, and God will place each soul in the realm for which he has fitted himself.

Can you imagine the disappointment and ache in the heart of Jesus to find in that day that so many have not valued His deepest fellowship enough to cultivate and build a life for it here and now? God does not arbitrarily say, "You go to heaven; you go to hell. You reign over ten cities; you are cast out. You may enjoy the kingdom; but you can't come in." That is silly and very unscriptural. Each soul determines his own destiny. The sinner goes to hell becauses he so chooses. The saint has or has not the rewards of fellowship and future association because he either does or does not desire it. The carnal Christian even though baptized in the Spirit may be saved, but miss the reward and glorious privilege Christ holds out for him.

He that is spiritual suffers the loss of *all* things that he may *know Christ* in the deeper and fuller relations. His garment is the Christian character wrought in him by the Spirit as he surrenders. *"Thou hast a few names even in Sardis which have not defiled their garments; and they shall walk with Me in white: for they are worthy."* Rev. 3:4.

Do not confuse the gift of salvation with character. No one experience can change you so you are thus qualified.

The prize is given to him that *overcometh*—not to him that is saved, or baptized, or is a great worker. Look at Rev. 2:7, 17, 26, and Rev. 3:12, 21. All this relates to the saints overcoming and thus qualifying—not to a sinner's getting saved.

In the face of this message there comes a *challenge* to any Spirit-filled saint. Could God hold out to us a more lofty and glorious life? One encouraging feature I find among spirit-filled folk is the hunger and desire on the part of so many for something *more* than the initial teaching of salvation, Acts 2:4, and the general line of truth given to babes in Christ. God has given us a wonderful and more responsible message. By His grace let us enter more fully into the *power* of its meaning. These are *preparation days* and He is AFTER US—His people.

We are looking to Him and long for His return but remember the scripture, *And His wife hath made herself ready.* The days are trying and God is leading His own into trials and testings and is faithfully disciplining the souls who *dare* and *love* Him enough to *die* and let go the natural, thus to *live* in Him and discover the joy and wonder of a walk with the adorable Lord.

20.

THE SPIRITUAL PURPOSE
AND ITS ATTAINMENT

LIKE to know *what* I am doing and *why*. I must have design or purpose in what I do. This I have in the simplest matters of daily living. Some I know are not constructed so, and life to such is generally a series of accidents or unrelated circumstances; there seems to be no purpose aside from the physical existence and getting through.

Very often in the transfer from the old life and creation over to the new, we are still conscious of characteristics of the natural. They may form patterns for the new life to fall into. We need to be careful here. A careless habit of the old life may ruin the flow of life in the new order and hinder the fuller manifestation of God in our lives. Sometimes it may be desirable to carry a desirable trait or habit along. For instance, I have noticed people who in childhood and youth have been thoroughly disciplined. They have learned the value of obeying promptly and yielding quickly. When they come into the walk of the Spirit, this background is of great value and saves them many a difficult jolt.

In life I like to know (as far as possible in God's will) what I am doing and why. In this wonderful new life, God does not leave us in the dark and expect us to stumble along and get through the best we can. Life is more than being good and getting to heaven. I am sure He wants us spiritually minded in this matter of living. The Christian life is not a series of disjointed affairs or an ordeal or even a song through which we pass. There is a definite purpose for which we were each created.

This divine purpose is like a vision toward which we move. In our make-up according to God's creative touch, we are all made to follow a vision of some sort or pattern. All life and activity is due to motivation toward some *desired* end or purpose. That is how we are *made* and is basic in our constitution. This is seen in the most simple and prosaic doings of life. With some the whole purpose rests in the realm of the material, and life is governed and colored by it. Others have caught a vision of spiritual purposes and meaning to life and so are living (right now) for eternity.

If some of us did not have some perspective concerning prophecy and know something of God's plan in unfolding His general scheme, we might develop a bad case of jitters. None of us is saying, "What in the world is the matter?" We are able to trace His hand in the signs of the times and so to intrepret the movements in the world. We are not worried thinking God has failed or Christ has failed.

Christians many times fail (and their faith is harmed) because they try *so* hard to accomplish things that God has no idea of doing. Instead of doing all sorts of good things (not wicked) but not in His will, they should find *His* will and walk in that. What a revelation to some hearts to find that after all the prayer, struggle, hard work and effort they fail to realize their purpose—all because it was *their* idea and plan and not God's! So in our Christian living if we do not have a spiritual, worthwhile purpose we shall make a great failure. *"Where there is no vision, the people perish: but he that keepeth the law, happy is he"* (*Prov.* 29:18). This verse is a great favorite with our missionaries. But I think it has a broader teaching than that usually given: that where there is no vision (no Christ or gospel) the people perish (or are lost).

It means that but much more. So we will let our dear Christian workers use it and get the vision of Christ to all they can. And you know I am a missionary in heart and would have gone to the field long ago only God had other plans for my life. In my college days I was a member of the Student Volunteer Movement and hoped to go. But God kept me home to train others to go. So now I go by proxy in the lives of many dear young men and women whom it has been my joy to train; and today they are serving in all different fields of the world.

Let us read not only the first part of this text, but the second part as well, *He that keepeth the law, happy is he.* I do not think the law here relates to the Ten Commandments. He is rather teaching us a principle of Christian living, and suggests the *power* of beholding or not beholding a vision and the *law* governing the same. After all, the law is cause and effect. Failure, loss, defeat, and tragedy are not just a happenstance—or accidental. There is always a cause back of it all—a law. So the text tells us: *happy,* or most fortunate, is one who discovers it and abides by it.

A more careful translation of the text from the original Hebrew will help us here—"Where there is no vision, the people *cast off restraint.*" How suggestive! Now we see why the loss is evident—there has been a casting off of restraint. The vision has *power* to restrain or to constrain in your life. Many times it becomes positive in its constraining ministry. Do you remember Paul in this position— *"The love of Christ constraineth us"?* And as to restraint: *"The Spirit suffered them not"* (*Acts* 16:7).

We do or refuse to do (in the matter of conduct) because of the power of the vision. Now we see more clearly the force of the verse. Where there is no vision (no restraining or constraining power in life), the people cast off restraint, and of course there is loss and failure. The objective and purposes have *not* been realized or attained. So there is loss, and life does not come to fruition. The design or pattern is not filled out. But most fortunate or happy is the one who discovers the law underneath the matter. Knowing this principle, he will order his steps accordingly.

Concerning the purpose or vision in Christian living, I want to give you a few Scriptures. *"Whether therefore ye eat, or drink, or* whatsoever ye do, *do all to the* glory *of God"* (1 *Cor.* 10:31). *"And whatsoever ye do in word or deed, do all in the name of the Lord Jesus, giving thanks to God and the Father by Him"* (*Col.* 3:17). *"If any man speak, let him speak as the oracles of God; if any man minister, let him do it as of the ability which God giveth: that God in* all things *may be* glorified *through Jesus Christ, to whom be praise and dominion for ever and ever"* (1 *Peter* 4:11).

From these texts we are able to see off in the distance a divine, supreme and spiritual purpose—the *glory* of God. In fact, the *glory* of God is the supreme purpose toward which the whole creation moves. Let us remember that God is a supreme Being. He is a dynamic, living personality. The first vocation of personality is expression, and this is a necessary characteristic of God. He continually desires to move *out* and express Himself. It is a fixed function of a living Being. Therefore God never hides Himself within the confines of His own nature.

This power to express and move out is found in the whole universe. It is found first in God's creative mood.

The order of angelic beings, ministering spirits, moves to His glory. The whole celestial realm declares the *glory* of God. All His creative power and design in life move on to the *glory* of God. So when we read these texts touching upon His glory as the purpose in life, we see *why* even the commonplace, ordinary acts of life are blessed with great dignity and may bear a mark of distinction. Why? Just because He has so planned. Think again of *motives* in your living and service and be encouraged to know it is His glory that gives life dignity—and beauty, strength and godly character.

We must keep in mind that all spiritual living is, after all, not dependent upon certain blessings and emotional reactions, but the whole structure rests upon divine unchanging principles. These are fundamental and basic, giving stability to the structure whether it be an individual life or a Christian assembly or church. Thus the fact of spiritual law governing in the building or erection of this wonderful divine life must be duly recognized.

Were we as sincere and careful in the matter of spiritual purpose as we are about material ends, I am sure we should grow in grace and save ourselves many a spiritual headache.

Why not study His Word and tarry long enough in His presence to find the purpose toward which He is working? Then we can trust Him to make the necessary adjustments in our spirit to help us in *living* to His *glory*. Were we once able to see this and *brave* enough to let God *reduce* our many activities and doings and what not, life would take on *spiritual values* and God would be glorified. I am sure it would *not* be *according* to the general design made by the human wisdom or even *religious* desires, but it would fall into a divine pattern, and His will and the glory of God would color even the most uneventful life.

Man's creation was unto the glory of God and He has *not* changed the original purpose.

Now let us consider a little *how* this glory or purpose may be realized. How may such a lofty, idealistic scheme be made a reality? God has not left us in the dark here.

Many times we get confused and erect all sorts of natural or religious standards for living and measures for gauging our lives. Thus we become involved with details, technique, and side issues. We try to *do* so many *things*. We forget that *all* He wants of us is to do *His will*. Let Him shape the pattern as He sees good. It is *His will* which becomes the *divine method*. Every life should fall into a divine pattern governed by *His will*. That would not make all lives alike but a marvelous display of glory would be reflected in each life by each one's doing His will. His design for you may not be *like* mine, nor mine like my brother's. But all will reflect His glory. Too many quarrel over their patterns and designs instead of surrendering *quickly to His will*, and *flowing* into them, and thus really *living*. Accept life, don't quarrel with it! Offer it freely to Him and let Him focus your living to His glory; and live, just *live*. Folks are trying to *do* almost anything else but *live*.

The *divine method* is doing His will. The doing of His will (great or small) always glorifies Him.

By way of illustration to show us a Scriptural picture of this teaching, let us look at the life of Christ. We know He kept the glory of God ever before Him, and spoke of it and related His life to it. It was the *motto* of His life. *"Then said I, Lo, I come: in the volume of the book it is written of Me, I delight to do Thy will, O my God: yea, Thy law is within My Heart"* (*Psalm* 40:7, 8). So, long before He reaches Calvary we find Him as the *ideal man* doing God's will.

Again we find this truth revealed in the Old Testament offerings. You will remember the order of them. The *first* is not a sin offering. No, it is *toward* God, and is a picture of Christ (the ideal man) *doing* the *will* of God. No mention of blood, sin, or atonement. It is the *will of God first*. Isn't that beautiful? God first! Even Christ in life, as told in the meal offering, has God's will first. So Christ emphasizes the great necessity of doing God's *will first*. Run through the Gospels again and note this. John 4:34; Matt. 26:42.

Now let us turn to an incident in His life showing the other side of the question—the glory or the purpose side. You remember very well the story of Jesus' raising of Lazarus as given in John's Gospel. Many times we read purely from a traditional standpoint and so miss anything fresh and inspirational in the bit we read. We have a certain mental attitude or approach and *knowing* the story from so many readings, we *anticipate* the climax and are thus blessed or thrilled. I am trying to read the Gospels afresh (and not to anticipate too much), but rather keep open to the Spirit to lay emphasis or throw light on some of the least expected portions, and I am charmed to find the Word opening up like a beautiful flower.

I was reading this story and waiting to reach the thrilling climax—*"Lazarus, come forth,"* but as I *tarried* the Spirit helped me to see *so* much even *before* I reached the usual point of victory. My heart and mind had been flooded for days with the thought of God's glory as the great purpose, and back in my mind was this atmosphere and condition. I was not directly conscious of it but I am sure *God was*.

How many of you who are familiar with this incident can recall Jesus' *first* words in relation to the situation? Let us review the story. The sisters are overwhelmed and are lamenting the fact of Jesus' absence. Lazarus is dead. Jesus is away—miles away, and on top of this distress He remains away two more days. What a very unhappy, depressing and tragic situation! *How* do they react? In the *natural* (note this, in the natural) they are so conscious of things seen that they are completely localized and seemingly have lost faith. They see Lazarus dead and in a tomb, and that sealed. They are tomb conscious, dead-man conscious, and are bound to the immediate and the death side of the situation. What are they *thinking?* "Oh, our dear Lazarus is dead, what *shall* we do? Oh, if the Lord had *only* been here! If He *only* knew our situation!"

Oh, dear soul, have you a Lazarus dead and laid in a tomb? Has some precious hope died on your hands and so you have had to bury it? It became so very annoying that you *had* to. Some idea, plan, hope, dream, ambition has failed (in health) and died. It is even *sealed* in a tomb. Are you, too, saying, "Oh, if the Lord *only knew?* Listen, my dear brother or sister, do not stay so *near* the tomb! You become tomb conscious, dead-man conscious, stone-over-the-tomb conscious and thus too local, too bound. You thus lose *perspective* of thought and vision. Do you not see how it affected the dear souls here?

What are the *first* words Jesus utters as He is fully aware of the *whole* situation—dead man, tomb, and the tragedy of broken hearts? Listen, *"When Jesus heard that, He said, This sickness is not unto death, but for the glory of God, that the Son of God might be glorified thereby."* Isn't that wonderful and beautiful? What is Jesus doing? He has faith, perspective of thought and vision, clear sight as to the *purpose,* and so *relates* the whole thing to the *glory* of God. What a miracle! He is able to *relate* tragedy, death, loss, and failure, all to the glory of God! Hallelujah! Praise God forever!

Here is a blessed secret. He *refuses* to be influenced by the shadow and gloom of a sepulchre. The dead man inside (all very real) did not disturb Him. His far-sighted vision carried beyond all this and found a resting point in the *glory of God.* What a lesson! Can you today interpret your Lazarus or your tomb in the light of the glory of God? If you are a Christian, and your life is dedicated to God and His will, you will see again in this light the force of Rom. 8:28, which is the same teaching. Could we all do this (and faith were manifest) what an unfolding and display of God's power we should witness!

But people are *bound* by sense perception. They are Lazarus-conscious. Jesus refused to be held under the limitation of anything seen. He *related* things properly. Yes, related even death and a tomb (the absolutely impossible) all to the glory of God. O, faith, thou glorious means of reaching, help us to see the *desire* and purpose of God! Teach me to relate, in this Lazarus-hour of my experience, the tomb to God's glory, and anoint my eyes to trace God's leading over the pressure and through the distress until I may see God's glory! Jesus does this all through His life and ministry—always looking *away, away,* away to God and His glory—ever *relating.* See Him dealing with a blind man. John 9:3. Here blindness is related to the works of God and thus to His glory.

In the wonderful 17th chapter of John we find the Lord's Prayer (really), or the High Priestly prayer. Usually we are occupied with the portions which have bearing upon *our* lives and relationships. We like the portions dealing with *"Thou gavest them Me; and they have kept Thy word,"* also the *unity* of verses 9 and 10, *"They are Thine. And all Mine are Thine, and Thine are Mine,* etc., and delight in what I call the *divine entanglement.* As a rule we are interested in the portions which offer personal appeal. But let us go back to the *first* part of the prayer. With what is He *first* concerned? Nothing less than the glory of God. It is a point to ponder—*"glorify Thy Son,"* and now listen! Verse 4: *"I have glorified Thee on the earth."* Isn't that wonderful! The *first* matter of value—the *glory* of God. "I have glorified Thee on the earth." The next phrase or thought is, How? "I have finished the *work* which Thou gavest Me to *do."* Isn't that clear and sweet? *First* was the glory of God. How? By doing His will, *"the work Thou gavest Me to do."*

Shall we not get our bearings in this matter of spiritual living? Some are so at sea. I find many misfits in life. Why? Often it is due to desires, plans, ambitions, and schemes (good and often *very* religious) but *not* spiritual or related to God's will or purpose. Sometimes a dear soul forces his or her desire and plan upon *another's* life and he tries so hard to make a go of it just because it is to him a splendid plan. Many, many times God is not within a million miles of it. And he has a terrible time using the promises, trying to *make* God do things He has no intention of doing, for they do not relate to His purpose at all. Life need not be a tragedy. Do not quarrel with life, *accept* it. Then offer it to God and let Him relate it to His *will* and purpose. We may not *enjoy* all the phases of it—often we *endure,* but as long as we find life and its doings *contingent* upon His will, we can live.

Stop long enough for a spiritual adjustment and much of the friction will pass away. The dead man in a tomb was *contingent* upon the will of God in purpose, and faith was needed to thus relate it. Let us take a little inventory of life. *What* is the real purpose and objective toward which you focus your living? Is it cluttered with the details of *doing* this, that, and the other? Are you bound by a technical aspect? *Not* so much the doing. All the doing must *relate*. Do less and have it properly related, and life will take on spiritual proportions and color. God does not thank you or reward you for doing a thousand things (good and religious) which do not relate to His will. Seek His will—do *that* and you cannot but glorify Him.

BROKEN  BREAD

John Wright Follette

If you mention the name of the late John Wright Follette in many Christian circles, you are certain to start a discussion about the man and his unique ministry. He was widely known as a Bible teacher and preacher. His writings continue as an extension of his God-given ministry.

In 1911, after receiving the Holy Spirit baptism, he was ordained by the Council of Pentecostal Ministers at Elim Tabernacle, Rochester, New York. He later became a member of the Assemblies of God. For many years he taught at the Rochester Bible Training School and at Southern California Bible College.

His writings have appeared in numerous magazines and books. *Arrows of Truth*, another book of messages and poems, is also published by Gospel Publishing House.

Of Huguenot ancestry, Follette was reared in New Paltz, New York, where he died October 3, 1966.

However, advice and counsel from the heart of John Wright Follette lives on in the pages of this book. The author was concerned about all who aspire to the ideal of Christ-likeness.

Wrote Follette: "Jesus Christ came not only to die but to teach us how to live. He desires to help us translate our problems into opportunities for high living. I cannot work and earn salvation, but I can apply myself to intelligent and spiritual living and build a character."

Gospel Publishing House
Springfield, Missouri 65802
ISBN 0-88243-474-8